Transformed by The Presence

Enlightening Experiences with a Unique Himalayan Master

Rudra Shivananda

Alight Publications

2021

Transformed by The Presence

By Rudra Shivananda

First Edition Published in December 2021

Alight Publications
PO Box 277
Live Oak, CA 95953
http://www.alightbooks.com

Transformed by The Presence © 2021 by Runbir Singh.

All rights reserved. No part of this publication may be reproduced, stored in a retrieval system or database, or transmitted in any form or by any means electronic, mechanical, photocopying, recording, or otherwise without the prior written approval of the author or publisher.

Softback ISBN: 978-1-931833-56-7

Printed in the United States of America

Myriad Salutations to
The Presence beyond the mind sea
Eternal Master that transforms
myself to Self, being to Be

Table of Contents

Foreward by Yogiraj SatGurunath Siddhanath / 8
Preface / 9

Part 1: The Seeker
Meeting Master / 15

Childhood Days and Growing Up / 18
  The Fragrant Harbor / 21

The Power of Heroes, Myths and Gods / 29
  The Path of Mysteries: Gods and Demi-Gods / 32

Puberty and Sexual Energy: spiritual inhibiter / 35

Schooling: Community and Service / 38
  Education / 41

Herbal remedies on the Path - Kundalini awakening / 50
  Herbs and Yoga / 52

Work / 55

The Path of Religion / 59
  The Sikh Dharma / 60

Taoism and Taoist Yoga / 64

The Path of Spiritual Practice without a SatGuru / 68
Dzogchen / 72

A Turning Point / 74

The Path of the Householder / 77

Highways, Sideways and Byways - diversions on the Path
    Western Astrology / 86
    Vedic Astrology / 87
    Gemmology and Jewelry Making / 92
    Reiki or the system of Usui Healing / 94

The True Kriya / 96

Part 2: The Practitioner
My Master /102

Spiritual Practice with a SatGuru / 104
    What is in a name / 105

Practice - Abhyasa / 107
    Nothing seems to happen? /113
    Perseverence in practice /115

First USA Retreat with Master - Breitenbush /117

Arriving Home - visiting Master's Ashram / 120

Spiritual Experiences during Pilgrimages
    Palini - Lord Muruga / 127
    Chidambaram - Tirumular /129
    Ekalinga-ji - Lakulisha / 134
    Gauri Kund - Gorakhnath Temple /135

Master's Revelations
    Master disappears into sunlight /139
    Master disappears in a black hole / 140
    He comes from the stars / 142
    Master and Babaji / 143

Master on Healing / 147

Master manifests in the Sun and the Moon / 148

Pilgrimages / 151
    The Presence of Gorakhnath / 152
    Ascent to Jwala Mukhi / 154
    Master and Shirdi Sai Baba / 157

Purifying the heart and tame the wild beasts / 161

The foundation of yoga - Ashtanga / 163

Spiritual Awakening / 166
    Stages of Transformation / 168
    Signs of progress in pranayama / 170
    Transformation - stages of spiritual practice / 172

Dispassion - Vairagya / 173
    Non-Attachment / 176
    Don't let fear rule you / 180

Jnana Yoga - Advaita Vedanta / 182

The power of Kundalini / 184

Ad-Hoc Parenting / 186

Practice and work tradeoff / 188
Personal Transformation / 189

Part 3 Acharya
Seva / 134
Expanding horizons and breaking barriers / 196
    First Hamsa Website / 196

Organizing events / 197
Advertising / 198
Editing and publishing / 199

Acharya / 201
  Experiences as a Teacher / 202
  Spiritual Evolution / 210
  The impact of Experiences on the Kriya Path / 212
  Spiritual experiences - A practical perspective / 214
  Experiences and realizations - a deeper perspective / 216
  Grief / 218

Siddhanath Yoga Parampara / 220
  The Healing power of the Sun / 221
  Siddhanath Kriya Yoga / 225

Guidance on Kriya Yoga / 227
  Is Kriya Yoga a religion? / 227
  Do you need to be a vegetarian to practice Kriya Yoga? / 228
  What about habits like smoking and drinking? / 230
  Self-Inquiry and self-Criticism / 230
  Is it dangerous to raise the kundalini? / 231

Guru Maa / 232

Master's Programs in USA / 235
The Ashram / 238
SatGurunath's contribution to Yogic Sciences / 241
Master's Many Manifestations / 241
The Uniqueness of SatGurunath / 242
The Presence / 246

More Books by Rudra Shivananda / 248
About the Author / 249

RUDRA SHIVANANDA
(alias Rumbir Singh Randhawa)

Perseverance is the magic of success so goes the yogic saying and Rumbir is the perfect example of this quality. So essential a quality is this that without it yogic advancement comes to a standstill. My connection with him stretches back to a past life in India to the nothern regions of Punjab. At that time he learnt from me the ancient science of Nath Yoga, and belonged to a kshatriya family related to my own.

I met Yogi Rumbir in the year 1993 at Los Gatos, California. He came and got initiated into the Babaji Kriya Yoga according to the Nath tradition. His constant and steady mind free from all emotional flux was not attained by sudden flight, but the result of past lives of ups and downs which he conquered and to eventually enter the realms of steadfast meditations. By his selfless work, service and meditation, he has for himself the hard won gold of a blissful meditations. A depth of understanding to serve humanity as ones larger self, and to transform himself by daily Dhyana more & more to consciousness. In my experience a tolerant and steadfast soul the types of which is rare to find.

May God Bless his Soul.
Alakh Niranjan
Yogiraj Gurunath

Foreword by
Yogiraj SatGurunath Siddhanath

Preface

Over the years, many fellow brothers and sisters on the spiritual path have asked me about my experiences with my Master, Yogiraj Gurunath Siddhanath. They have also been curious about my background and my experiences prior to meeting my SatGuru. In the back of my mind, there was always the idea that I should really write some of these things down instead of just talking about them. However, there was never enough time and too many other matters took priority.

The past year has been one of the strangest for humanity, with the world-wide shutdown due to the Covid pandemic. It was the first time in almost thirty years that SatGurunath did not come for a tour in the US. It was the first time in twenty years that I did not visit his Ashram near Pune, India.

Even as I sit down to write this, the terrible strain on humanity is still going on. There is at this time a huge medical crisis in India and much suffering. Although the situation is better in the US with a much higher rate of vaccination and lower new cases, it is still no time for complacency. My prayers go out to all those suffering and all those who have passed from this world.

Personally, in the midst of all the Zoom sessions during the last year, I have had the blessing of time to introspect and revisit some of my life experiences. It seemed to me to be the right time to work on a book about my spiritual journey in gratitude to my Master's abundant grace.

The book is divided into three parts. In the first part, called the Seeker, I mostly explore my life before meeting SatGurunath. There are two chapters, one at the beginning that I share my first meeting in this lifetime with him and a second chapter that is called 'The Turning Point', where he appears to guide me thirteen years before

I physically meet him. Most of the first part is about my early life experiences as well as the different spiritual paths that I had explored.

The second part is called 'The Practitioner' and most of it is about my mystical and transformative experiences with SatGurunath. There are also chapters on his primary teachings. Some of these experiences may seem subjective, but keep two factors in mind: that many other students have independently recounted similar experiences and that these are significant to me because they had an impact on my own understanding and spiritual realization.

The third part of the book is called 'The Teacher' and briefly explore my experiences in service to Master and as a teacher in Siddhanath Yoga Parampara. I've also included some of the student guidance that can shared and will be helpful to all spiritual seekers.

My writing style is generally to have short chapters of a few pages on a particular topic instead of knitting a few topics together into long chapters. I keep mostly to that style in this book. I also like to group together related topics, and this can lead to temporal jumps, that is breaks in chronology. Since the focus here is on life experience, I have made abundant use of photographs. They speak volumes and can help to explain what I want to convey in the fewest words.

To give the reader a taste of my experiences with SatGurunath, I have used a few paintings and some photoshopped images to represent my visions but they are inadequate and can only give an indication of their impact on me. Sprinkled here and there are also short semi-poetical musings that percolated in my mind while attempting to organize my thoughts and memories.

For the rest of the book, I have decided to use the term 'Master' instead of referring to SatGurunath's various titles, because that term best conveys the relationship of Master-disciple as well as the masterful wisdom and power that he transmits by his very Presence.

I have included a handwritten forward from Master. He had given this note to me back around 2003, when I showed him the first book that I had written. He said that I will know when I should use it. After eighteen years, it occurred to me that this is the right place for it.

Master has many admirers, devotees, students and disciples. My spiritual adventures with him are by no means unique and many others have shared their experiences with me, but I am only able to recount what I have personally experienced. In the same way, I've shared a few of my photos with Master and with fellow Hamsas to illustrate or augment the narrative.

My focus in this book has been on the spiritual experiences and their effects on me. There is very little about Master's human side - his sense of humor, devotion to his family, and his love and patience for his students. I don't talk about what food he likes or the sports he watches with us, or the jokes he makes. Such details although fascinating, have been omitted because they don't directly relate to his spiritual mission.

Master is like the sun and shines on all of us and does not give preferential treatment to just a few. Everyone can tune in to him and receive his blessings.

It is my sincere hope that the reader will gain an appreciation for the uniqueness of Master's Presence through this biographical offering and be moved to further avail of him for their benefit and that of all of humanity.

Om Shanti

> Guru's grace awakens me from illusion's dream
> Guru's grace leads me across samsar's stream
> Guru's grace transforms me to Hamsa supreme

The Seeker

Seek your radiant Self
Set forth now, find the Presence
That Master that shines bright over the world
Him that awakens your eternal light

Awakening to awareness
Day and night, selfing to Self
Merge in that Light that lights all lights

Meditate to purify monkey mind
Live purely to pacify desires
Live a loving life free from strive
Mindful in work and play

Be the full moon
Come out behind the cloud of ignorance
Shine as the sun at noon
Immersed in soulful silence

Part 1
The Seeker

Figure 1
Master at Los Gatos Satsang

Meeting Master

My knees were not aching anymore from the hour or so of sitting on the floor without a cushion, but my back was suddenly stiff and my heart center was being pushed back a few inches against the wall. Even though I was stuck against the wall and could not move forward, I was calm and peaceful and felt very much alive. This was not how I imagined the evening would go when I had decided to drive up the steep roads of the Santa Cruz hills near Los Gatos for a "spiritual talk" or Satsang with a Himalayan Kriya Yoga Master.

The day before, I had been searching through the East West Book Store on Castro Street in Mountain View. It was my favorite place to spend a couple of hours. I would usually go there on the weekends but I'm not sure why I decided to go on a Thursday after work. Most of the staff was from the local Ananda Community which I had come to know because of the Kriya Yoga workshops and initiations in their headquarters in Nevada City. I said hello to them and decided I would only spend half an hour before driving across the Dumbarton Bridge to go back home for dinner - I was already late but this was before the advent of cell-phones, so couldn't warn my wife. There was a bulletin board for posters near the restroom which I wanted to visit, but a quick glance stopped me in my tracks.

There was a really bad and dirty photocopy of a page sized poster – it looked like it had fallen on the ground, stepped on and later picked back up and tacked on the board. What attracted my attention was image of Babaji, the Immortal being who guides the spiritual evolution of humanity and is the heart and soul of Kriya Yoga. As I looked further, I was shocked to feel a strong attraction to the image of an Indian Yogi that was below the image of Babaji. This yogi was apparently in the US and giving his teachings. In the past, I had always passed by the opportunity to meet so-called Masters from India because I just did not feel any connections, but this time it was different. I was not exactly sure why, but I was determined to meet him.

When I got home, I called the phone number that was on the poster and was informed that there would be a Satsang the next night and was given instructions to a private home in the Santa Cruz mountains. I arrived there before sunset and met the organizers – a couple who were hosting the Master. There were three or four others there and we were showed to an upper room and waited for the yogi to show up.

A short while later, the Master entered, sat on a large, cushioned seat and greeted us. I was feeling very strong energy transmission from him even before he came in and then it ratcheted up when he started talking. About forty-five minutes into the talk, he started telling us that he was really there to give us spiritual experiences which only a true Master would be able to do and not just impress us with his words. He was only there to give us Shaktipat – a transmission of spiritual energy, akin to a kundalini awakening. It was also a healing energy transmission.

He asked us to focus on receiving his Shaktipat at the heart center and that was when I started to be pushed back towards the wall. It was powerful demonstration.

After the talk, I asked to meet with him and requested his initiation into Kriya Yoga. The main purpose of the Satsang was that we should practice Kriya Yoga to achieve Self-Realization. He asked me about what I was doing, and I explained to him my spiritual practice at that time. He said it was a good start but that he would give me a stronger and more advanced Kriya Yoga. I agreed to come back the next morning was given a personal initiation into Kriya Yoga. It was the beginning of a series of personal initiations into different Kriya techniques that the Master blessed me with over the period of two weeks. This was an unusual course of events – he would normally require a student to practice the basic Kriya techniques from the first initiation for a year before giving more techniques.

The reason he made an exception in my case was because I was already practicing the second and third level Kriya techniques that I had received from Paramahansa Yogananda through the Ananda teachers. Master corrected and improved my understanding of the basic and advanced techniques over that summer. It was a life changing experience for me.

Now, it was strange that I did not recognize Master from my earlier experience with Padmasambhava but because of everything that had happened in the intervening twelve years, it was not in my conscious mind and was only a forgotten memory. A few years later, the memory re-surfaced while I was packing up some of my Tibetan books and I saw an image of Guru Rinpoche. I was stunned to remember that the image that had replaced Padmasambhava in my meditation so many years ago looked very much like Master. It was a revelation of how he had reached out and altered the course of my life even before we physically met.

For whatever reason, I was reluctant to discuss this event in detail with him, but when next we met, I told him that I had experienced that he was closely related to the great Padmasambhava and he smiled knowingly and said that was so.

I have given that experience in a later chapter called 'The Turning Point.'

Childhood Days & Growing Up

There was nothing extraordinary about my childhood, apart from a feeling of being alone and different, brought about by being thrust into an alien landscape where I looked totally different from all our neighbors - an Indian born among the Chinese.

I was naturally introspective and kept to myself. This tendency was reinforced by my being the first-born child and waiting over two years before welcoming a sibling.

Hong Kong in the early 1950s was a city in upheaval, barely recovering from the Japanese occupation that only ended in August 1945 and struggling with the large numbers of refugees trying to escape the mainland chaos. Both my parents had suffered through the occupation and were married in their late teens, as was the custom.

My father worked as an engineering apprentice in the Waterworks Department and was assigned housing near where he worked in the Wanchai district of Victoria Island. Our home had two rooms - the bedroom where all of us (there were five of us and our parents) slept and a family room where we had our meals, listened to the radio, or played. The kitchen was separate, as were the bathroom and toilet. There was no running water for the bathroom, and we would have to carry the water from the kitchen sink - this was especially interesting in Winter when we had to heat the water first, before having our old-fashioned bucket bath.

Early memories include being chased by a neighbor's black Alsatian whenever I wandered out of our home. Another exceptionally sharp memory from when I was three or four years old was, one night, being put on my grandfather's lap and while he forced some whisky down my throat to temper his grandson and prospective warrior - the burning sensation put me off on liquor for almost sixty years.

This may have helped re-inforce my inclination towards becoming a spiritual warrior rather than a physical one.

The most frightening experience was going to the toilets which were outhouses. This was especially true in the dark when all manners of cockroaches, lizards and spiders would frequent the place. Hong Kong had tropical summers with torrential rains and a very dry and cold winter in those days.

A reason to bring up these little trivia is because they partly defined my childhood mind. The greatest challenges were alienation and fear which I had to deal with on a constant daily basis. I had to develop courage just to go to the toilet or to play outside. The toilet helped to train me to squat well and not to waste time while the alien environment helped to sharpen my awareness and introspection.

When I was six, I started grade school and had to take a tram as well as walk about a mile every morning. Every day was an adventure among the milling populace of the busy and bustling island.

School was challenging socially since I was an Indian in a predominantly Chinese society, but I learned to adapt and spoke Cantonese fluently. This grade school was also diverse because it was the one school in the colony that catered to the small Indian population and offered a language option for Hindi. Unfortunately, the Hindi teacher recruited from India was a horror and delighted in jangling his keys in his pocket and then throwing them at students who displeased him. Of course, the Chinese students would gang up on the non-Chinese and I found myself often defending against bullies who delighted in pulling off my turban. Thankfully, by the time I was ten, I was head and shoulders taller than my classmates and had developed a mean right hook. They stopped trying to test me.

It was also around this time that Death reared its awful mark and set in motion my life-long search for the meaning of life, for there is no greater motivator than the imminence of one's own mortality or the touch of death on those who are near and dear.

One day, I came home and was told by my tearful mother that my grandfather had passed away the night before from a heart attack. A strange feeling came over me - a brief dissociation of my mind from my body and an internal voice cried out 'WHY?', before I succumbed to tears as well, for I had been very fond of my grandfather despite the whiskey incident. I set my youthful determination and vowed to discover the mysteries of live and death. However, being only ten or eleven, it was soon forgotten or put aside for I had not the tools nor means to move forward.

About two years later, I was once again shocked by my mother revealing that one of her brothers had been in an accident and had passed away. This maternal uncle was very dear to me because he would play with me often and had patiently taught be how to ride a bicycle. I was confused and refused to believe that the universe would take away such a nice person who was only in his early twenties - it did not make sense. Who decides such things? Is there someone in charge or was this just some stupid random game?

I was now determined to pursue answers and had even found the tool for my research - the Hong Kong Library.

> The material man moans and mourns
> O Death, Wait, Wait, it's not time yet
> I have made much in this sojourn
> More, more, much more to be done yet
> Death's stern gaze dash hope forlorn

The Fragrant Harbor

As I write this, I feel nostalgic about the former British Colony, Hong Kong, in which I was born and lived for the first nineteen years of my life. Memories bubble up uninvited – some welcome, others not so much. A lot has changed in the last twenty years there, lots of turmoil and unrest. But then, it had been like that ever since its beginnings.

The island was a small village of fisherfolk when it was ceded to the British after they won the First Opium War with the Manchu Ching Dynasty of China in 1842. Missionary schools were soon setup to help educate the small Chinese population. Interestingly, one of the first graduates from the local medical school in 1892 was Sun Yat-sen who later toppled the Ching Dynasty and established the first Chinese Republic in 1911.

My parents were children when the Japanese occupied the colony for three years and eight months - a time of great privation and tribulation. Although they did not talk much about those times, I was aware that at least one of my grand-uncles and a few other relatives had been executed during the waning days of the occupation.

After World War II, the population was round 600,000, but the influx of refugees from Mainland China forced to flee the communist take-over inflated the population to two million by 1955. This of course strained the infrastructure to breaking point.

As a kid, I was ignorant of the undercurrents. My memories were more about playing in the streets with other boys. We played marbles, a primitive version of game cards based on Chinese heroes and divinities, but my favorite pastime was flying kites. We would put bits of glass on the kite string and engage in destructive battles in cutting each other's kites strings, with the concomitant heartbreak and tears of running after one's favorite kite that had been liberated.

My home was close to the Cathay Theatre and there would be crowds coming and going at certain times. There were not enough new movies so most of the shows were very old movies and I was able to sneak in with some of the other boys when the theatre workers would turn a blind eye to our shenanigans. Some of the newer ones were in Cantonese and a majority were in the format of the traditional Chinese Operas. Most of the actors and actresses were opera stars. It was only in the 1960s that I was exposed to the Shaw Brothers martial arts movies.

There were also some unpleasant memories. There were the droughts that affected the colony during the 1960s. Even though it was an island surrounded by sea water, there was a perennial shortage of drinking water. There were several years, where for weeks at a time, we were restricted to four hours of water every four days. We had to bring buckets and barrels to specific neighborhood taps and fill up the best we could. Our family was in a better situation than the majority of the population because we actually lived within a Government Water Works facility and so we had better access and were able to get water sometimes in between the four days.

There were natural disasters such as typhoons (hurricanes), flooding and landslides. I remember looking out from a window and seeing a tall building sliding down a hillside.

My most traumatic memory of that time was from 1967, when the mainland Cultural Revolution spilled over to the colony. There were daily riots and marches by communist sympathizers punctuated by exploding bombs hidden in shoe boxes and left in public areas. I had a ring-side seat to the demonstrations because my high-school was near the Governor's Mansion as well as the US Consulate. During classes, I could see and hear the chants from the rioters flaunting their copies of the little red book – the sayings of Chairman Mao.

During the same period, the very foundation of the colony was shaken by the bombs and communist agents shouting anti-British slogans. They wanted the British to leave. It was the first time that

I'd started hearing my elders speak not so softly about leaving for other countries because the Red Army was going to march in any moment. It was a very fearful time which lasted too long but eventually petered out when the movement on the mainland was overthrown due to the displacement of large population groups and the decimation of the old guard taken away to the re-education camps.

It was a tumultous time in the world also. I would watch the evening news and learn about the dire situation in Vietnam and the anti-war demonstrations outside the White House. However, my only experience with Americans at that time was of the American sailors who would periodically inundate the seedy parts of Wanchai, nearby where we lived. That was the area of the notorious Suzie Wong Bars. Normally, they would be active at night when I would not be going out, but occasionally I would see them lying passed out on the streets when I went to school early. My thought at that time was that they were going to get a large laundry bill to keep their whites spotless. This was before I was enlightened by my friends that the sailors were not just getting drunk. This was a shocking revelation for a teenager.

I was exposed to Western music and songs on the streets as well – the local teas shops each had their own phonograph and vinyl collection. They would play Elvis Presley and Paul Anka, among others in the late 1950s and early 1960s. In the mid-1960s, these tea shops had almost disappeared but there was still one that hung on and that was where while walking home, I heard the song "San Francisco (Be sure to wear flowers in your hair)." The song struck a chord within me, and I decided that I would go to San Francisco one day. I kept walking by the tea-shop to listen to the song for over a week.

Figure 2a
Where I was born:
Queen Mary Hospital

Figure 2b
Where I lived as a child

Figure 2d: Harbor Scene

Figure 2c
Cathay Theatre

Figure 2e
Street scene in Wanchai

*Figure 3a
Refugees fleeing
to
Hong Kong*

*Figure 3b
HK Peak Tram
Tourist View*

*Figure 3c
Wanchai Bar Scene*

Play of Time

When I was young and filled with hope
I set out to find the way
Following the light of knowledge
My mind shone bright
My path was in sight

At midday I was lost
Illusions clouded my vision
Unsure footsteps faltered
Until Master's light appeared
Then darkness disappeared

In darkening dusk
Why cower in fright?
Let's fight the night with spirit's might
Stare down death's sight
Divinity my immortal right

Figure 4
Play of Time

With Father, Uncle and Grand-father

With my mother

I liked playing in the bushes

Figure 5: With family members

The Power of Heroes, Myths and Gods

When I was eleven years old and in grade five, our main class teacher decided it was a good idea that we should learn more than was given in our regular textbooks by borrowing books from the library. In those days, the only library was that at the city hall in the Central District of Victoria Island. The reason he wanted us to learn more was that there was not sufficient space in the secondary schools (grade seven to grade eleven) to accommodate all the students from grade six. Out of over thirty thousand grade six students, only about six thousand could progress to middle and high school. Therefore, there was a colony-wide test that every grade six student had to take and only the top six thousand could move forward to grade seven. The rest of the twenty-four thousand had to go to work or get into a trade school of some sort.

I had never been to the Central District but was able to get the directions from my father. It was quite terrifying to take the tram and then walk to the city hall among all the noise and people, but somehow I made it and then went up three floors of the building, only to find out that I needed a library card before I could take out any books. The staff helped me fill in a form to get two cards - each card enabled me to borrow one book. It is not possible to describe my joy when I was allowed to browse the books in the three floors of the library - a whole new world was opened to me, a world of knowledge that was previously denied me.

Instead of focusing on the books that would help me progress on my next educational level, I was determined to use the opportunity to discover the meaning of life in the shadow of death.

In my search for something meaningful, I grasped at the books about heroes such as Hercules, Theseus, Perseus, and Gilgamesh - those who were demi-gods and whose actions seem to elevate them further to the level of divinity. I spent the whole summer immersed in the study of the Trojan War, the venerated tales of Greek civilization - the clash between the Greeks and the Trojans. It was amazing to read about the gods who fought for one or the other side. My favorite character was Odysseus who was the king of Ithaca because of his wisdom and counsel, as well as being the central character of the 'sequel' to the Iliad, called the Odyssey.

My fascination with these mythical stories was due to fact that I saw them as allegories to human situation from an elevated or expanded perspective. It seemed to me that there must be some deeper message in the stories about Heracles (Hercules) whose tragic life was made meaningful by the performance of the twelve labors. Was he a solar deity and the labors a metaphor for his traversing the twelve signs of the zodiac as has been suggested by some occultists? There could be multiple layers of understanding for such powerful myths. The ancient sages gave us myths to learn and live by but seldom gave us the keys to the mysteries involved. Only those initiated by these Masters were given the sacred secrets.

The great heroes such as Perseus who slew the Gorgon Medusa and defeated the sea monster to rescue a princess or Theseus who slew the monster minotaur and founded Athens all had great appeal to an impressionable young person looking for something greater than one's lonely and fearful life. A favorite author of mine who modernized our understanding of myths, Joseph Campbell, wrote about a hero's journey as one of spiritual growth into one's ultimate being in the book called 'The Hero with a Thousand Faces":

> *The agony of breaking through personal limitations is the agony of spiritual growth. Art, literature, myth and cult, philosophy, and ascetic disciplines are instruments to help the individual past his limiting horizons into spheres of ever-expanding realization. As he crosses threshold after threshold, conquering dragon after dragon, the stature of the divinity that he summons to his highest wish increases, until it subsumes the cosmos.*

> *Finally, the mind breaks the bounding sphere of the cosmos to a realization transcending all experiences of form - all symbolizations, all divinities: a realization of the ineluctable void."*
>
> -- Joseph Campbell, The Hero with a Thousand Faces

Of course, at that stage in my life, I was more enamored with the romance and adventure of the hero than Self-Realization, but I think the spiritual background provided meaningfulness to the adventure and gave some satisfaction to my yearning far more than I was aware:

> *The usual hero adventure begins with someone from whom something has been taken, or who feels there is something lacking in the normal experience available or permitted to the members of society. The person then takes off on a series of adventures beyond the ordinary, either to recover what has been lost or to discover some life-giving elixir. It's usually a cycle, a coming and a returning.*
>
> -- Joesph Campbell, The Hero with a Thousand Faces

A fictional hero who fascinated me that summer was Tarzan of the Apes, created by Edgar Rice Burroughs. An orphaned baby left in the jungle, Tarzan is the archetypical hero for every young person who has ever yearned to be brave and strong, to stand face to face with death and rescue loved ones from dire conditions just in the nick of time. Tarzan was not just an adventurer - he is a Janus like character who on one side could tap into his animal nature and defeat his enemies in the jungle and on the other hand can deal with civilization and the demands of being a human being. In his books, although writing as a pulp author, Burroughs dealt with the threat of death and its inevitability. His characters overcome great odds, never giving up, but always living by a moral code. It was fascinating.

There were only a couple of books by Burroughs in the library, but I wanted to read more and so discovered tiny used book stalls in Central as well as Causeway Bay and developed a life-long love for old books. I was able to pick up some more paperback Tarzan books and immersed myself in them.

However, summer does not last forever, and I found myself having to take the Secondary School Entrance Examination with the rest of the grade six students all over Hong Kong. It was a stressful day for everyone - students and parents and then we had to wait several weeks for the results. These were printed in the South China Morning Post so that we could find out about our fate.

Thankfully, I passed and was accepted into a very prestigious high school, called St. Joseph's College, one of the earliest schools to be founded (1875) in the colony. It was run by the Catholic teaching order of the La Salle Brothers. I was told by the principal during the interview that I was the first Sikh student who had been accepted into the school.

The Path of Mysteries: Rama, Gilgamesh, Heracles and Tarzan

During my formative years, myths were an important part of my spiritual journey. I always had an intuition that there were many spiritual truths hidden in these stories and that if I could decode them, I would understand life better. Later on, I found in my research, information about the Greek and Egyptian mystery schools that taught various mystic truths. These also helped to consolidate my ideas about the world and the meaning of life.

One of the first movies that I recall watching when I was four or five years old at a local theatre was a version of the Ramayana - the epic story of Avatar Rama. One of the most memorable scenes that I can still remember after more than sixty years was when the "monkey" devotee of Rama, Hanuman, set fire to the city of Lanka by growing his tail to a length beyond imagining and swinging it around to spread the flames. I remember cheering and clapping.

When I was older, I felt that Hanumanji represented some type of power, maybe pre-human type from our evolution. Perhaps, this type of power could be harnessed within each and every one of us. I did not know about the life-force energy prana yet, but would listen on the radio to stories of Chinese heroes who could fight by utilizing an internal energy called Chi, and so connected Hanumanji with that internal power.

When I was about twelve, I read the stories from the epic of Gilgamesh, King of Uruk, a Mesopotamian demi-god and hero. In some of the stories, his only friend was this wild-man, Enkidu, who lived among animals and is hairy-bodied and muscular. Enkidu reminded me of Hanuman because he helps Gilgamesh to kill the sacred bull sent by Goddess Ishtar.

In the myths, the human and animal parts of us are generally represented separately but work together. In the modern re-telling, Tarzan seems to combine both aspects within himself. He can be civilized in modern society, but when he returns to the wild, he can unleash his animal self and literally become the king of the jungle. To me, there was a connective thread through all of these stories that caught my attention.

It is not my intention to go into details about the role of myths in forming my spiritual field before I embarked on the Kriya Path, but only to give a brief glimpse. I would be re-miss if I did not mention my fascination with Heracles, especially his twelve labors. Here was another demi-god who had performed incredible deeds.

I can only touch on the significance of the twelve labors. In this mystery myth, Heracles is the soul who has to journey through the twelve signs of the zodiac to learn some lesson or solve some karmic riddle in order to attain to true immortality and mastery of the Self. Each of these labors needs to be decoded and meditated on in order to receive the wisdom hidden within.

For example, the slaying of the Nemean Lion is symbolic of passing through the sign of Leo. In this myth, Heracles chases the lion into its cave, but the cave has two exits, and the lion would escape from one when he came in the other. Heracles had to seal one exit and then he had to fight with the lion without any weapons, only with his bare hands.

An interpretation suggested in the writings of the theosophists would be that the lion represented the individual ego, and the cave is in the brain cavity surrounding the pituitary gland which has an anterior and a posterior lobe. Heracles had to seal the posterior lobe which represents his emotional nature and utilize the frontal lobe representing his reasoning mind. This just touches the surface of the mystery of one of the labors. The initiate had to meditate and be instructed into all twelve of the labors.

Although while immersed in these myths, I was still too young and inexperienced to understand them, I always had an inner feeling that there were truths and wisdom hidden in them that would reveal the deeper aspects of this bewildering world. I made up my mind to unravel these hidden codes left by the sages of the past.

Puberty and Sexual Energy - Spiritual Inhibitor

As we reach our teenage years, all of us in some form or another will experience the power of the animalistic instinct for reproduction - the sexual drive and the concomitant hormonal cocktail that is released to drive away coherent thought or ethical considerations. I was a very confused teenager because nobody in authority, neither my parents or my teachers, had anything to say about what was happening to me. This was long before the introduction of Sex Ed class and there was no Internet to search.

My first introduction into the female form was naturally from an old Playboy magazine one of my classmates had pilfered from his father's stash and passed around in school. Unfortunately, it raised more questions than answers, but nonetheless was of great prurient interest.

Since I was in an all-boy's Catholic school, the only time we had to interact with girls was during social events organized several times a year with Catholic girl's schools. Obviously, there was a lot of pent-up frustration and awkward fantasies among the students. A lot of time was wasted in the pursuit of sexual knowledge among the tiny and dingy bookstores hidden in the alleyways in Central and Causeway Bay. Repression brought about feelings of guilt and fear.

During a particular difficult summer vacation, I discovered the writings of the Apostolic Fathers and saints in the library, and this brought about more confusion on what one was supposed to do with this particular energy in our lives. They basically taught that sex was either the Original Sin that caused the Fall of Man or was the direct result of it.

> *The original intention of God was for us to generate not by marriage and corruption. But the transgression of*

the commandment introduced marriage on account of the lawless act of Adam, that is, the rejection of the law given him by God. Therefore, all of those born of Adam are "conceived in iniquities," having fallen under the condemnation of the forefather. [St. Athanasius]

All of the writings counseled celibacy and the abolition of marriage as a means to achieve spirituality, Although, somehow, baptism and faith in Jesus Christ as the savior would take away the stain of the original sin, this was not enough for the really faithful, such as Origen, one of the greatest early theologians who is alleged to have had himself castrated to be a worthy follower of Christ. This sort of stuff was a lot to take in for a teenager.

While searching for books in the alleyways, I came across a very used paperback missing the front cover which was called *The Complete Illustrated Book of Yoga* by Swami Vishnudevananda. I had no knowledge of yoga but was attracted to it and the subsequent study and practice of the techniques within fostered my life-long dedication to the Hatha Yoga. There were exercises in the book that helped me to transform the sexual energy into spiritual energy, particularly the three bandhas. Even the asanas and basic pranayamas relieved a lot of the stress of puberty.

Of course, I had no idea what was happening when I was doing Hatha Yoga until some years later when I came across Elizabeth Haich's book *Sexual Energy and Yoga*. It introduced me to the concept that there are techniques to ease the sexual tension that builds up and that it was counterproductive for spiritual growth to unnecessarily deplete one's sexual energy.

During my time in college, I was led to explore Buddhist meditations that helped to overcome the mental compulsions that give rise to instinctual reactions. Coincidentally, there were helpful kundalini yoga techniques revealed by Yogi Bhajan that I found in the spiritual community in Berkeley. Unfortunately, I did not have access to these tools during my high school years.

It is by no means easy to conserve and transform one's sexual energy to a higher form of vital energy called ojas, but it is necessary for the raising of kundalini shakti, the nascent potential for divinity within each of us. It was many years yet before the proper tools and sufficient practice gave rise to wisdom and self-control.

According to the understanding and wisdom of my Satguru, it is harmful to try to repress the natural tendencies when they can satisfied without hurting oneself and others. There are many examples in religions institutions where those who have wrongfully taken a vow of celibacy are unable to maintain it and harm those under their care. There is great harm being done under the cover of orthodox hypocrisy. When one has developed the proper channel to transform the lower energies into higher forms, sexual desires will dissipate on their own.

During my adolescence, there was always a struggle between the desire for enlightenment and the desire to satisfy one's physical and emotional needs.

Let there be no regrets
Neither guilt nor fear to appear
Each night surrender to Divinity's might
At each dawn, give thanks to new day

Schooling - Community and Service

The environment at the all-boys Catholic school was very different from the primary or elementary school that I had navigated for six years. Besides the regular classes such as English, history, geography, science, mathematics, we had the addition of biblical knowledge, catechism and ethics. We had to memorize one book of the New Testament each year and would be tested on our knowledge of it. There were weekly quizzes and a mid-term exam as well as the final examination of the year. I will return to these topics in a future chapter on religion.

The culture of the school was vastly different in terms of discipline and focus and I intermingled with not just the majority Chinese students but also with the Portuguese kids, whose family had been going to the school since its inception. I also had to stretch myself to learn a third language - choosing between French and Chinese - I chose French and found myself learning not just the language but also the culture from our French teacher.

The colonial pyramid education system continued in that each of the grades 7 to 11 had five classes - A,B,C, D and E, with the lowest scoring students relegated to E, and the best students in A. At grade 10, there was a further delineation in subjects such that those in the A, B classes would have Physics, Chemistry and Biology and stop having subjects such as English Literature and History, in order to separate the science majors from the English majors.

At grade 11, all the students in Hong Kong had to take a Certification Examination, also called the O level Examination, in order to proceed to grade 12, and 13, because there were only three classes in these higher grades and then at grade 13, there was an A Level Examination or Matriculation where those who had survived the culling would compete for the scarce University places. Out of six thousand Grade 13 students, only about five hundred would merit to enter the University of Hong Kong. The most prestigious were the 150 that could be placed in the Medical School.

The reason I have described this system is because obviously, it made us extremely competitive and studying very hard at all times in order to get a chance to get into university level.

The teachings of Lord Jesus which we were made to study every day, together with the morning prayers such as the Lord's Prayer and Hail Mary, had a great impact on me, but that played out over time and at a later stage of my life. The most significant effect on me was the concept and practice of community service.

At school, as I managed the stuff we were forced to learn, I was able to join several extra-curricular activities such the Boy Scouts, the Chess Club and the Debating Society. When I was in grade 10, a couple of the more senior schoolmates recommended that I join the Interact Club, which was affiliated with the Hong Kong Rotary Club.

Interact is a service club that gives young people an opportunity to participate in fun and meaningful service projects while developing leadership skills and meeting new friends. The basic principle is to help others. It is about "service above self". Through service activities, we learned the importance of developing leadership skills and personal integrity, demonstrating helpfulness and respect for others, and advancing international understanding and goodwill. The St. Joseph's College Interact club helped to develop and carry out a wide variety of service projects. We would raise money for worthwhile causes, working directly with people in the community to make it a better place.

Learning from and working with the members of the club instilled in me the activity and experience of Seva, which I had heard many sermons about at the Sikh Gurudwara, but never realized. The concept of selfless work is a key driver of the Bhagavad Gita, the Indian Yoga classic:

Strive constantly to serve the welfare of the world. By devotion to selfless work one attains the supreme goal of life. BG 3.19

Every selfless act is born from the eternal infinite Divine, It is present in every act of service. Whoever ignores this law, indulging his senses for his own pleasure, ignoring the needs of others, wastes his life. BG 3.16

From the perspective of serving the Lord by serving humanity, Jesus has said: *"Whatever you did for one of the least of these brothers and sisters of mine, you did for me." (Matthew 25.40)*

In the three years that I was in the club, we were able to serve the community in a number of projects, the most notable three that I remember:

1. We raised money and bought a truckload of toys and gifts during Christmas and distributed them to children in the Kowloon Walled City, the ungoverned and dangerous enclave of the triad gangs. The laughter and joy of the kids still linger in my mind after fifty years.

2. We raised money and volunteered our services to paint and restore a ferry boat that was anchored and used as floating clinic for the indigenous boat people. It was staffed by doctors and nurses from Project Concern. It was joyful to watch the people lining to receive medical help when the clinic was functional.

3. We raised the money and volunteered our services to convert an elementary school's dirt playground into a concrete one. The school was in the rural Lantau Island in the district of Mui Wo. We spent over two weeks sleeping on the desks in the school rooms and taking our daily baths in the nearby river. We had to unload and manually carry the cement bags about two miles from the pier in the summer heat and then mix the cement using a small concrete mixer we had rented. It was hard work, but very satisfying when we completed it.

At that stage, I felt that selfless service was the path to self-realization and overcoming our fears and the tyranny of birth and death cycles.

According to *Shirdi Sai Baba: Selfless service alone gives the needed strength and courage to awaken the sleeping humanity in one's heart.*

Education

There seems to be a confusion concerning the current system in most countries for educating the young people. Whether to mold the new generation to mimic their parents or to evolve them into thinking and creative assets. The purpose of most societies is to develop their children into contributing adults and the yardstick to measure their level of contribution is the wealth they can amass without causing problems such as political agitation or criminal conduct.

Growing up in a colonial system dominated by Chinese teachers with their cultural values had some interesting side effects. One prominent one that affected my life for many years happened while I was in Grade 4. During this time, I was a precocious and studious child who would raise my hand in class whenever the teacher asked a question, and I knew the answer. However, I was puzzled that my fellow classmates never seemed to try to give answers in class, although many of them were very smart. I thought that they were just shy.

After the mid-term examinations and we were given our report cards, I was happy because I had come third in the class of forty students but was bemused when I read a comment from the main class teacher that my behavior was conceited and that I should restrain my enthusiasm. There was a firestorm when I showed the report card to my father – he was angry that I had gotten a bad behavior comment from the teacher, and I was actually punished even though I had done quite well in my grades. This somehow caused me to regret standing out and my young heart was hurt. From then on, I never raised my hand in class.

My parents wanted me to be a doctor and I was in the equivalent of the pre-med class during Grade twelve and thirteen – the goal being to get into the elite medical school in the University of Hong Kong. Unfortunately, I had discovered that I had no aptitude for the medical sciences since I abhorred reading about diseases and really didn't want to be surrounded by sick people all day long. My interest tended towards physics and mathematics, but my parents did not see any future for me in those disciplines. The consequence was that I immersed myself in philosophical or mystical books and neglected my studies. Naturally, I didn't do well in the biological sciences, but I did well in physics and mathematics. To please my parents, I told them that I wanted to be an electronics engineer. My plan was to study in the United States.

My bachelor's degree was a B.S.E.E. and I graduated summa cum laude. Interesting, the only class that I got less than an A grade in was a class called Advanced Engineering Mathematics. The professor would come into class and then start writing equations and solving them on an extremely long blackboard during the whole class and at the end of the class would give us some assignments. I found it boring and so I would start meditating with my eyes closed and focusing on a technique that involved the third-eye center in the brain. And of course, because of my primary school trauma, I never bothered to try to answer questions in the class. The consequence was that I got a B+ grade because of 'lack of class participation.'

My nature is to go deep into those topics that I am interested in.

After working for a few years as an engineer, for some inexplicable reason, I was made a manager and had people reporting to me and had to do things like budgeting, work performance reviews and other management functions that I was not aware of. I also sorely lacked people skills. Following my nature, I decided to enroll in a management class that was organized by the Hong Kong Management Association together with a local university – this turned out to be a multi-year course that turned into the equivalent of an MBA. It was fascinating.

Some years later, while I was working for a Korean technology company based in San Jose, I had to deal with a lot of intellectual property issues – the company was licensing a lot of IP from US companies to jump-start and complement their home-grown research and development efforts. I had to work with several attorneys that we had hired as well as negotiate with our partners' attorneys. The legal agreements I had to wade through were a mixture of legal jargon and technology buzzwords. IP law was coming into its own at this time. I was interested and decided instead of just taking some law classes, that I would enroll in a four-year doctoral course and earned a Juris Doctor (JD) degree. When I look back on the time and effort involved and all the evenings spent on studying law after work, it is amusing to review such obsessive behavior.

My love of learning also extended to my hobbies. When I became fascinated with gemstones, I studied and took the ultimate test for gemology and became a licensed gemologist.

It may be that my hobby is really a life-long love of learning!

There is no end to learning

Be satisfied with true knowing

Figure 6a
Grade 7
Class Picture

Figure 6b
Fund raising Fair at
St. Joseph's College

Figure 6c
Getting ready for community service - picture with Principal Brother James and Class Teacher Brother Lawrence

Figure 7a
Addressing a convention of the chapters of the Interact Clubs of HK

Figure 7b
Chairing an Interact Club meeting at St. Joseph's College

Figure 7c
On a boat to do community service on an outlying island

*Figure 8a
Landing in Mui Wo
on Lantau Isand*

*Figure 8b
Hauling cement from the
pier to the school*

*Figure 8c
Speeches by the local
councillors*

*Figure 8d
Ribbon cutting for the
new playground*

*Figure 9a
A retreat with fellow classmates*

*Figure 9b
High school graduation dinner*

*Figure 9c
Bachelor degree graduation photograph*

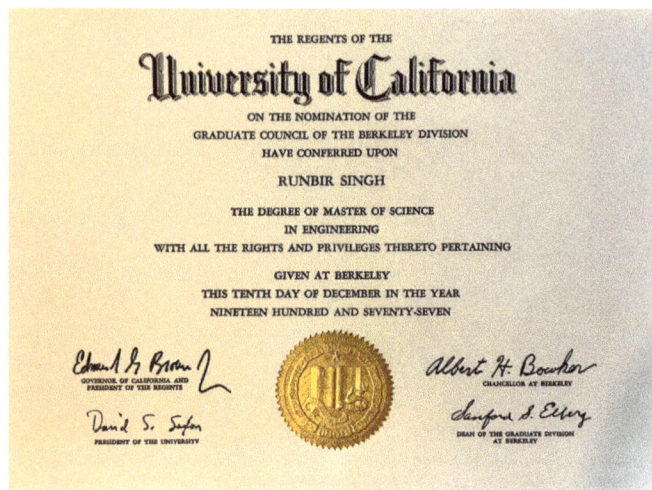

Figure 10a
Master's Degree

Figure 10b
FGA
Gemmological diploma

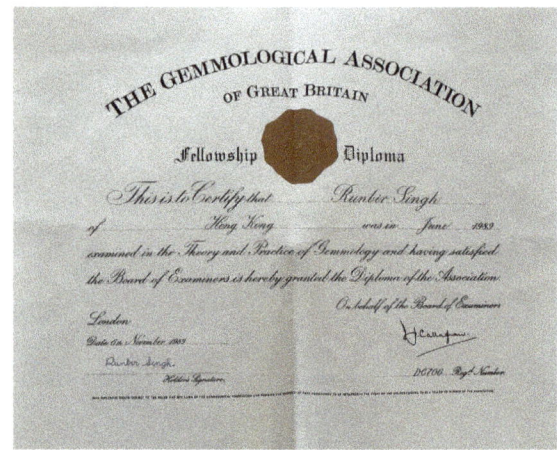

Figure 10c
Garduation for
Doctorate in Law (JD)

Figure 11b
Giving a speech at a jewellery conference in Hong Kong

Figure 11a
Working at a college library

Figure 11c
A farewell dinner with my Taoist Teacher in HK

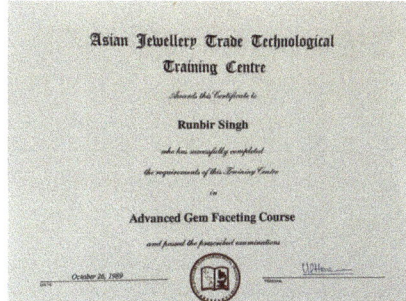

Figure 11c
A passion for learning

Herbal Remedies on the Path -- Kundalini Awakening Experience

The early 1970's were an eclectic time - especially in a place like Berkeley. I was exposed to many different types of spiritual paths, some traditional and some very "new-agey". Many of my friends used a variety of mind-altering substances - some just for the thrill and others in a genuine search for a way to pierce the veil of materiality that they perceived was hindering them from realizing some higher consciousness and experience of reality.

During this phase of my journey, I was not receptive to experimenting with any substances that would damage my mind - especially since I had travelled to California to get a university degree - I rejected LSD, peyote and other hallucinogens because they were not consistent with practices of self-control and mind-purification that formed my primary sadhana (spiritual practice) at that time. There did not seem to be any canonical reference to the use of herbal enhancements for meditation apart from a reference in Patanjali's Yoga Darshana. My Buddhist teachers neither approved nor disapproved of their use but my study of the scriptures, especially the precepts would seem to argue against any type of intoxicant that could lead to the loss of self-control.

However, it was almost impossible to escape from partaking of marijuana because of its prevalence amongst my friends and classmates. It was difficult for me particularly since I had never smoked anything before, and their fumes seemed to lessen the amount of oxygen in the air for me to breathe.

One evening, I had gone over to see a graduate friend who had an amazing music system, and we were going to listen to some heavy rock. He had just acquired a new set of Dahlquist floor speakers which were supposed to be amazing. After a beer, he offered me a joint and I decided to try it since everyone had assured me that it was a mild high and was not addictive. It turned out to be a powerful pivotal experience for me.

After a few puffs and mild coughing, I was able to inhale deeply and then felt myself dissociated from the body – a liberating experience. When the music was turned on, I felt my whole body vibrate and before I knew what was going on, I was rolling around on the floor, feeling every note as if my body was the instrument. A euphoric emotion dominated my mind and I started to laugh and continued to laugh non-stop for over an hour, according to my friend. He was getting a bit worried after an hour and stopped the music, much to my disappointment. I still continued to laugh and roll around for a further ten to fifteen minutes before exhaustion overtook my body and I fell asleep for a couple of hours on the floor.

When I woke up later, I felt my spine was electrified and there was a current flowing up and down continuously. It was disconcerting but being young and ignorant, I decided it was just some after-effect of the pot and went home to rest some more. The effect lessened over the next few weeks, but my body remained sensitive to any sound vibration for some time. My mind seemed to have achieved some sort of expanded state but I was not sure whether it was just some sort of delusion. Certainly, my meditation sessions seemed to go deeper with less effort.

Over the next few years, I had plenty of opportunity to smoke marijuana, but was not able to repeat the experience from my first time. Eventually, I found it was more of a hindrance than help in my sadhana as well as my studies and so dropped its use and just took a few shallow drags when offered by my friends.

After I graduated and moved on with my working career, I did not smoke anything for the next thirty years. Paradoxically, the next time I experienced marijuana was in a drink offered at an Ashram in India during a yogic ceremony in 2001. This was a herbal concoction that yogis use to celebrate a major festival in honor of Lord Shiva – a story for another time.

Herbs and Yoga

Years after my Kundalini experience, I had the opportunity to learn more about ayurvedic herbs and their use to enhance meditation.

Yogis have always been known as experts in the utilization of natural herbs for the prevention or curing of diseases, as well as for enhancing the yogic practices of their students. Agastya, the great Himalayan *rishi* who developed South Indian culture is also credited with instituting the *Siddha* science of herbs. The perfected yogis called variously *Naths* and *Siddhas* also originated the branch of *Ayurveda* (the ancient *Vedic* science of health and healing) called *rasayana* or path of longevity that included the practices called *kaya kalpa* or physical and mental rejuvenation. It is interesting to note that the *Vedic* science of medicine also uses *yogic* tools, such as *asanas* (physical postures), *pranayama* (breathing techniques), *mantras* (audible formulae of energy and power) and meditation as part of their system of healing. There is a close inter-relationship between Yoga and *Ayurveda*.

According to Patanjali, a great *siddha* and author of the Yoga Sutras, herbs are legitimate tools for becoming a *siddha* or perfected yogi:

> *The accomplishments (of perfection in Yoga) are the results of birth, herbs, mantras, intense practice and cognitive absorption.* Yoga Sutras IV.1

In more modern times, it was mentioned in Yogananda's spiritual masterpiece, "Autobiography of a Yogi," that Panchanon Battacharya, a Kriya Master and disciple of Lahiri Mahasaya, set-up a mission in Calcutta to teach Kriya Yoga and give herbal remedies.

Following Patanjali, it is important to note that herbs do not replace the other tools and factors, such as intense practice, for success in the path of Self-Realization. Additionally, the herbs are generally taken in conjunction with a healthy diet – it would be counterproductive to feed the body all the poisons of processed foods and meats from our mineral-depleted and junk-food culture, and hope for the positive effects of these transformational herbs. A healthy life-style without dependencies on habit-forming drugs and intoxicants, sufficient rest and sleep, is a pre-requisite for a strong spiritual practice that can benefit from the use of herbs

On the other hand, there are many herbs that have been used for millennia, with well-understood and documented effects. Many are also now widely available in *Ayurvedic* stores or on the Internet. Of the hundreds of herbs, there are especially five that can be considered by all practitioners of Yoga. They are *shanka pushpi, ashwagandha, brahmi, guggulu* and *shatavari*. They help in two ways, first by increasing the physical and mental immunity to diseases – if one is struck down by illness, then it is difficult to meditate. Secondly, they help to increase the capacity of the body and mind to be transformed by the yogic techniques. There is a sixth one that is very beneficial for concentration and getting ready for meditation, called Calamus, but it is rather difficult to get outside of India.

The following is a brief introduction to the benefits of the commonly available five yogic herbs:

Shanka Pushpi: This is for rejuvenation of the mind. It improves memory, concentration, and stimulates the development of creativity centers in the brain.

Ashwagandha: Often called the Indian Ginseng, it is the best healing herb for both body and mind. Physically, it strengthens the nervous and skeletal systems, that is the nerves, bones, tendons and muscles, relieving aches and pains in joints. For the mind, it is calming and can reduce anxiety and insomnia, promoting concentration and deep sleep. This is an excellent herb to aid in both the physical endurance and mental alertness required of long spiritual practices.

Brahmi: As the name suggests, this herb is used to gain knowledge of the Divine Creator. It helps to control anger and attachments, by calming the mind. It also stimulates certain parts of the brain to configure it for higher consciousness.

Guggulu: This is an excellent herb for longevity. It promotes flexibility of the muscles, ligments and bones for a steady and pain free posture. It also lowers cholesterol and strengthens the heart. It is a blood cleanser and also regulates blood sugar.

Shatavari: This is a good general tonic but specifically for countering fever, acidity and dehydration. It calms the heart and increases love and devotion.

These herbs are available in powder form, in capsules, or made into tinctures or even jams (often in combination with other herbs). It is easiest to take them in capsules or pills. If taken in powder form, then generally there will be directions to mix it with warm milk, honey or some other way, as they all are rather "untasty" for the normal palate.

Different physiologies will react differently to these herbs due to the human range of sensitivity. Each person will need to take responsibility for the use of these potent herbs. It is best to start out with a strengthening regime of *shanka pushpi* and *ashwagandha* for at least two weeks, before adding *brahmi* for another week, followed by a week of *guggulu*, and finally *shatavari*.

If the benefits are observed, without any undesirable side-effects, then a daily regimen of all five herbs should be taken for optimum effect. They will have a strengthening effect on all five bodies, the physical, energetic, emotional, mental and causal. I've put my personal experience with herbs here rather than in a later section because it seemed to fit the subject matter.

Work

When finishing my graduate studies, I did not get enough funding to pursue a doctoral science degree. This was not a problem as I was looking forward to some practical work in the engineering field. After visiting a few of the Bay Area companies, I discovered that the pioneer semiconductor company, Fairchild, had a facility in Hong Kong and it actually had an opening for an engineer with microprocessor-based assembly language programming as well as analog circuit design knowledge - basically a combination of hardware and software expertise which I happened to possess. So, I returned to Hong Kong and started my work career there.

Although the project work that I engaged in was remarkably interesting and challenging, my primary goal was to make a living and save up money to pursue my spiritual studies. I did not try too hard to impress my superiors and let my work speak for itself. To my surprise, I was continuously promoted and at the end the five years, I was the engineering manager responsible for over a hundred engineers and technicians.

Unfortunately, in 1982, the company decided to close down their Hong Kong facility and move to the Philippines. Although offered a management position there, I decided not to take it because I did not want to re-locate my brand-new family. It was not difficult for me to move to another company and that began a series of different companies that I would work for an average of five years each. My talent for communicating difficult technical concepts into simple understandable language made me popular with salespeople and I began a career in marketing and business management.

My work required a lot of traveling outside of Hong Kong and I had to travel throughout Asia as well the US. The upshot was that I had very little time for spiritual practice, since I had to balance family and work responsibilities. This became somewhat better as the children grew older but by that time, I had returned to California and had also met my Master.

It is not an easy matter to choose a line of work that does not affect one's spiritual growth and also can provide enough money to support a family. I am amazed to think back how easily such opportunities appeared to me.

During my more than ten years working out of Hong Kong, there were opportunities to deepen my Buddhist meditation practice as well as explore the Taoist path. Most of these practices were preparatory and purifying and were very useful when I finally stepped on the Kriya path.

I would take any break time and practice breathing or mindfulness techniques. One of the best techniques for stress release and awareness training is a being mindful with the breath. Sometimes I would do this with eyes closed, but there were times during tense meetings that I would practice with eyes open but slightly defocused. The technique is to become aware of the breath coming in through the nostrils with the inhalation and then leaving the nostrils with the exhalation. After a few minutes, I would start to count the number of breaths from one to ten and then down from ten to one. Even five minutes of this practice will clear the mind and increase awareness.

Figure 14a
HK Scene of Kun Tong with the Fairchild Bldg where I worked in the middle

Figure 14b
My work area inside the building of Fairchild Semiconductor (HK)

Figure 14c
Receiving an award from the COO of National Semiconductor during a Sales and Marketing Conference in Bangkok

*Figure 15a
Making a customer presentation*

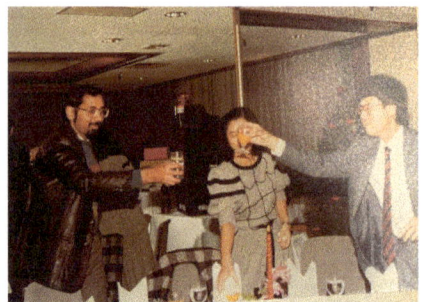

*Figure 15b
Toasting during a customer dinner*

*Figure 15c
Hiking with colleagues*

*Figure 15d
Sleeping on the hillsides*

*Figure 15e
Watching sunrise on a peak in Lantao Island*

*Figure 15f
Team building exercise- with staff*

The Path of Religion

I was born into a Sikh family. My father's life was centered on his religion and he eventually became the President of the local Sikh temple or Gurudwara. Every morning and night he would do his required prayers. My mom, although born in India, was brought up in Hong Kong, and was more eclectic in that she was devoutly connected to the Boddhisattva Kuan Yin and would go to the Chinese temples whenever she could in addition to the Gurudwara.

Sikhism is a relatively new religion founded by the saint Guru Nanak who lived in the Punjab of the 1500's. He was a devout Hindu who taught through his poetic chants the highest philosophies of the scriptures in the simplest manner and in the local language to the common folk of his time. He attracted a following and when he passed on, his teachings were carried on by his appointed successor. A Sikh was a seeker of the truth, a person on the path to the Divine. This went on for several hundred years until the tenth teacher, Guru Gobind Singh, who could not find a worthy successor, appointed the Sikh bible, called Guru Granth Sahib, the definitive collection of all teachings from the Sikh Gurus and other enlightened teachers, as the representative Guru. In Sikhism, Guru is God and God is Guru. It seems that the Nanak Panth was a sect of the Sanatana Dharma, or perennial tradition of Bharat (India), but Guru Gobind Singh founded the Khalsa or The Initiated, The Pure, those who have faith in and uphold the tenets of Sikhism. Over time, it became a separate religion because of political and economic reasons.

Going to the Sikh Temple was a weekly burden for me because I felt it was a waste of time to sit for three or four hours listening to talks by people who seem to me to quote passages from the Guru Granth Sahib that proclaim great ideas, but then end with political proclamations or denunciations of other castes or creeds. The 1960's were a very divisive time and eventually led to the great debacle in the storming of Golden Temple of Amritsar (the most holy site for Sikhs) in 1984. In 1967, I made a stand and refused to go the Gurudwara. This caused a great furor and rift with my father, but we compromised, and I agreed to go on specific festive days only. Only many years later, did I come to appreciate the great wisdom contained in the Sikh teachings of devotion and service. In my teenage years, I tried hard to escape from it.

The Sikh Dharma

As I have mentioned, Sikhism is a fairly new religion founded by Guru Nanak Dev, who was born in 1469 in the Northern Indian region of Punjab. It was a very turbulent time with continuous invasions by the Muslim rulers through Afghanistan. There was a lot of suffering among the population and the primary religious trend was towards devotion to deities. The people took refuge in the teachings of the great saints rather than to the rituals of the Brahmin priests. Nanak was the leading saint of the time and his tradition was the Nanak Panth, that later developed into the Sikh religion after a succession of nine Gurus. The tenth Guru did not appoint a human successor and instead chose the accumulated teachings of the previous nine Gurus as well as other contemporary saints which collectively is called the Adi Granth was the perpetual Guru on earth.

The word Sikh has the meaning of a spiritual seeker and is derived from the 'shishya' or disciple or learner. A Sikh is one who believes in the unity of God, the teachings of the ten Gurus and the Guru Granth Sahib. The three pillars of the religion are: meditation/prayer, honest living and sharing one's wealth and happiness with others.

The daily practice consists of reciting or reading five prayers every day – three prayers in the morning, the fourth in the evening and the fifth at night before sleep.

From a practical perspective, when I was growing up, my parents would take us to the Gurudwara or Sikh Temple every Sunday. I enjoyed the Guru-banis and kirtan – the chanting and singing of the teachings, even though I did not understand much of it. What was boring was the talks by the temple leaders – these were mostly of a political nature. We all looked forward to the prasad (blessed sweet) given at the end of the service followed by the langar (communal feeding). The food was prepared by volunteers - my father being one of them. He was great at making dahl, the spicy lentil dish.

From a spiritual perspective, as a young person, what I could understand was that we should get rid of our humai (ego sense) and obey the orders of God (hukam). How this was to be accomplished was a mystery to me. We just had to do our work properly, look after our fellow beings and read the good book. It was not until many years later, when I revisited my spiritual roots that I gained a much deeper understanding of the profound and unifying Sikh teachings.

The most sublime text that a Sikh would study is the poetic Japa Ji composed by Guru Nanak. The Japa Ji is composed of the Mool Mantar, two slokas and thirty-two pauris. It is the path towards God Realization and by following the pauris or ladders, one step at a time, one can ascend to the abode of God (sacha khanda). The goal is to become a Karam Yogi – combining Karma Yoga, the yoga of action, Bhakti Yoga, the yoga of devotion and Gyana Yoga, the yoga of knowledge. This sounds technical, but all works from devotion.

This is in accord with the highest teaching of the Bhagavad Gita, the unsurpassed yogic text of Sanatana Dharma. However, Guru Nanak was speaking to the householders of medieval India whereas Krishna was addressing the royal clans five thousand years ago.

In order to stay in the abode of God, one should build a house (that is, our body-mind complex) composed of the following virtues -

control of faculties that lead to equilibrium of mind, knowledge of scriptures that give wisdom, worship of God that leads to love of mankind. Only then does one take the role of jivan mukti or liberated soul.

In my youth, although I loved to listen to the Japa Ji, I was more attracted to stories about his eldest son, Sri Chand. Guru Nanak's mission was wholly dedicated to helping householders reach God and so he did not support the ascetic style of life adopted by the yogis and saints of his time, who were the siddhas under the Nath sampradaya, founded by Gorakhanath. However, his son Sri Chand adopted the celibate lifestyle and became a Nath yogi, in contrast to his father's teachings. Father and son approached God from different lifestyles.

Sri Chand had great devotion to Guru Nanak and founded the Udasin Sampradaya, a monastic order that taught yogic meditation but revered the Granth Sahib, the words of the Sikh Gurus. Sri Chand actually travelled throughout India and preached the message of Guru Nanak.

There are many miraculous stories attached to Sri Chand. While I was a child, out of all the Sikh paintings around the house, the one that I was attracted to was the one about Sri Chand and how he preserved the blood-line of his father by rescuing his nephew from prematurely going to heaven. Figure 12c shows him rescuing the boy.

Although, I had never heard of the Nath yogis at that time, when I moved out of my parent's home, I requested to take that picture with me. I felt a great connection to the person depicted and only many years later, realized his connection with Babaji.

*Figure 12a
Sikh Temple
in HK*

*Figure 12b
A wedding ceremony
inside the Sikh Temple*

*Figure 12c
A painting of Shri Chand that
I cherished since my
childhoold days*

Taoism and Taoist Yoga

Being brought up and spending my first eighteen years in a Chinese society, I was heavily influenced by Taoist ideas. Although I did not cultivate (practice) deeply, there are certain virtues and techniques that have been ingrained in my spiritual practice. I have also found many similarities betwenn the Taoist Alchemical schools, the Siddhas of South India, and the Naths of Northern India.

The roots of Taoism is in the shamanic traditions of central and southern China. Over thousands of years, many different schools have developed. There has been influence from Buddhism from India and the local Confucianism. Just as Chan (Zen) Buddhism is attributed to an Indian monk, Bodhidharma, who travelled to China, there are also stories about Lao Tzu, the author of the Tao Te Ching (a seminal Taoist scripture) being Indian or the Nath yogi Boganath taking the role of Boyang.

The existing major schools are:

- Magical Taoism: The way of power
- Divinational Taosim: The way of seeing
- Ceremonial Taoism: The way of devotion
- Internal-Alchemical Taoism: The way of transformation
- Action and Karma Taoism: The way of right action

My interest naturally gravitated to the Internal-Alchemical path. This has also been called by some people as Taoist Yoga.

The major ideas of Internal Alchemy:

- In the formless and undifferentiated Tao, our primordial state had no form, no mind, no body, no sense, no feeling. We were not subject to death, growth or decay.

- In the state of duality, Yin-Yang, the father and mother energies come together to break or separate us from Primordial Tao.

- In the womb, the internal energy of the fetus is still undifferentiated. At birth, this pristine energy is separated into three parts: generative (ching), vital (chi) and spirit energy (sheng). There is also a separation of body and mind.

- As a person grows older, generative energy is dissipated through sexual activity, vital energy is lost through emotions, and spirit energy is weakened by mental activity. This loss of energy leads to sickness, old age and death.

- We can recover our energies through internal transformations, attaining health and longevity, as well as returning to the original undifferentiated state of Primordial Tao.

- Slowing down the aging process in order to achieve immortality.

My own experience with this path was mostly on the foundation practices such as Chi Kung, Tai Chi and chi circulation such as microcosmic orbit. The major obstacle was the difficulty to get trained by a true Taoist Master and the secrecy surrounding the higher practices.

By the time I was ready for the middle stages of cultivation, I had met Master and no longer had the time or energy to pursue the Tao in this way.

To put things into perspective, I can share the transformation stages in this internal alchemy. There are many subsects that offer different kinds of training in each stage, but the intended results are common among them:

- Beginning Stage: Building the foundation
    - This is divided into external strengthening and internal

strengthening. The external strengthening works on the physical body structures. The techniques are tendon-changing, massage, and internal martial arts such as Tai Chi Chuan. The goal is to revitalize the skeletal system and attain external physical health

- o Internal strengthening is accomplished by movements of the spine and some forms of internal martial arts
- o Refining the mind: The goal is to attain a level of disinterest in excitement and sensual stimulation, minimizing desires, and eventually, stilling the mind. Techniques are different forms of meditation

- Middle stages: Transforming internal energy

  - o Gathering, refining and transforming sexual energy. Energetically, most of the work is done in the abdominal area, called the lower tan-tien. In the mental arena, regulating and minimizing sexual desires is required
  - o Ching is transformed into vital vapor (Chi) which is collected in the chest area, called the middle tan-tien
  - o Refined chi becomes sheng which is collected in the upper tan-tien in the third-eye center
  - o Pathways of the microcosmic and macrocosmic orbits are activated

- Final stages: completion

  - o Returning the spirit energy to the void
  - o Emptying the mind of thoughts, dissolving the duality of subject and object; attaining a state of emptiness
  - o Emergence of the seed of Tao; formation of the immortal fetus; birth of the immortal body

- Cultivating the void to merge with the Tao

The completion stage of this internal alchemy is shrouded in mystical language and only high initiates have an opportunity to touch on it.

The time of secrecy is coming to an end and there have been efforts by Taoist Masters to spread the teachings of their ancestors to a wider group. The first was semi-recluse Master Wang who taught me the basics in Hong Kong.

Another group and its leading expert that I had experience with was The Healing Tao founder Master Mantak Chia. He gave many workshops in Berkeley during the early 1990s that I was able to attend. His books are invaluable resources for those who are attracted to this path.

The lasting lesson from my studies in Taoist yoga is not concerned with techniques or philosophy. It is the natural harmony with nature. Observing the seasons and the ebb and flow of life.

The Path of Spiritual Practice without a Sat-Guru

My first experience with a spiritual practice was with Vajrayana, the Tantric Buddhist path from Tibet. I had practiced Hatha Yoga from the books of Vishnudevanda and Yogi Ramacharaka, as well as Yogi Bhajan, it was only when I visited the the Nyingma Institute in Berkeley founded by Tarthang Tulku Rinpoche that I began to understand the concept of a comprehensive program of spiritual practice for achieving higher states of consciousness and beyond.

I perceived that the difference between the spiritual path and the religious path was that relying on the scriptures based on the experiences of others was just the stepping-stone to one's efforts and discipline to achieve one's own experience.

However, at that time, I was determined to succeed on the path without taking a SatGuru or Spiritual Master. This may have to do with my Sikh upbringing which inculcates the faith that God is Guru and that human beings are not reliable guides unless they are like the first ten Sikh Gurus. Additionally, I think it was primarily because it was not yet time for me to meet Master.

One important way teachers differ is how much authority we give them over our practice and life. In the Theravada tradition, the teacher is an elder who guides us, trains us, and inspires us by their example of following the eightfold path. In Mahayana schools, such as Zen/Chan, the master is likened to a powerful and skilled doctor who does what has to be done to cure our spiritual illnesses. In Vajrayana Buddhism, the teacher is a guru. Tantric gurus are seen as manifesting enlightenment mind in this world for our benefit, and through our devotion we discover that their mind and ours share the same enlightened nature. That's the theory at least, but personality and teaching style are also important. In practice, a Theravada elder can mind your business as fiercely as any Zen master, and Tantric gurus can be the very embodiment of gentleness.

Embarking on a course of Buddhist spiritual practice, I was given a Tibetan name, after I made the Bodhisattva vow and took refuge in the Buddha, the Sangha, the Dharma and the Primordial or Root Guru, who in this case was Rinpoche, Padmasambhava, the great Guru who established Buddhism in Tibet and subjugated the negative energies of the land.

There were two sets of practices – the outer preliminaries which came from the sutra path and the inner preliminaries coming from the tantric path. The following is a brief description of these practices which I engaged seriously in for over five years and then sporadically for another few years after I married:

The outer preliminaries:

- The opportunity of a human birth – due to the karmic cycle of birth and death, we take birth countless times. Sometimes, as lower forms of life and sometimes as higher forms. Only when we are in the higher forms can we truly engage in spiritual practice that can lead to liberation from the samsaric cycle (birth, death and suffering). The human birth is a rare opportunity to have the requisite consciousness to achieve nirvana and so we should strive to make the most of this life and not waste it on creating more obstacles on the path through our desires and actions.
- Meditation on impermanence – it is evident from our experience that nothing lasts, but we still act as if we can keep these passing moments of happiness. In order to internalize the reality of change, we meditate on how all the worlds and even our sun has a finite existence. Then we look at the lives of great beings, of emperors and conquerors – where are they now? Finally, we can examine our own body, emotions and mind to watch the passing show.
- Cause and effect of actions – this is an abstract meditation. First, we would examine the ten non-virtuous actions that

cause suffering and the ten virtuous actions that produce pleasure. Briefly, there are three physical non-virtues – killing, stealing and sexual misconduct; four verbal ones – lying, divisive talk, harsh words and senseless speech; three mental ones – covetousness, harmful intent and wrong views. One should examine each of these and examples of such activities to understand them. The next part is to examine the effects resulting from action. There are four effects – the first is called fructification, that is, it is a karmic summary and effects the whole life, such as being born in a hell; the second type is similar to its cause such as if one lies, then one would be slandered by others; the third type is environmental such as a killing cause can lead to being re-born in a place where life cannot be easily sustained; the fourth type is a cumulative effect, that is, the effect is spread over several life-times. Meditation on virtuous actions is also needed.
- Suffering – after meditating on the faults of cyclic existence, that is, the karma wheel of life, and contemplating the different existences such as plants, animals, heavens and hells, we would examine the sufferings that are inherent in them. For instance, even gods have a finite existence and towards the end of the lives, they are shunned by other gods because they start to lose their luster - they start to smell bad and lose their divine fragrance and suffer the thoughts about their coming re-incarnation.

The inner preliminaries: the goal for these exercises is to repeat one hundred thousand times for each.
- Taking refuge with grand prostrations – the tantric refuge is in the Guru, the Buddha, the Dharma, and the Sangha. From a standing posture, one kneels and with palms together, one spreads out to lie flat on the ground to recite the refuge. Standing up, one repeats this grand prostration a number

of times. I usually do fifty rounds and sometimes up to a hundred rounds which is quite a heavy exercise even in my twenties.
- Generating Bodhicitta (mind of enlightenment): this is a mind of compassion in which one cultivates the intention to help all beings attain freedom from suffering. In this practice, one cultivates first equanimity to develop even-mindedness. We inherently have a bias to love our friends and hate our enemies. Only by removing the poles of attachment and repulsion can we further develop love and compassion for all beings. Having developed compassion for the suffering of sentient beings, we can move on to generate joy for their happiness and good fortune now and in the future.
- Vajrasattva meditation – a purification of the mind. It is said that our very own non-virtue prevents us from achieving the vision and realization of profound meaning of suchness. Before engaging in the visualization of the Buddha Vajrasattva, one should mentally examine past non-virtuous actions, generating contrition for them. Then one commits to refrain from these non-virtues. Only after that should one visualize the complete enjoyment body of Vajrasattva residing on a lotus above one's crown. Then, the one-hundred syllable mantra is recited at least twenty-one times.
- Cutting attachment – we offer our most precious possession, which is our very own body. One would visualize a dark goddess holding a skull in her left hand and a curved knife in her right. In this meditation, we would visualize the goddess emerging and cutting off our heads so that we observe our own headless corpse. It is rather intense.
- Guru Yoga – this practice can a method of generating ultimate cognition, entering a state of blessed empowerment. One begins by visualizing the environment transforming into a pure land. One becomes Vajrayogini and the object of meditation is Guru Padmasambhava. A mandala is visualized and made into an offering. The mantra of Guru Rinpoche

is recited as well as many others. There is a merging with the Padmasambhava which transforms us. Finally, there is dissolving into empty space. After some time, one offers a dedication of the fruits of the practice to the benefit of all beings.

A lot of time and effort is needed to cultivate these preliminary meditations. However, I'm told that even realized and accomplished lamas value these practices and will continue them. They have profound effects on our mental field.

The bottom line is that no matter which system you have chosen, the mark of spiritual practice is:

perseverance - just do it and keep doing it until realization.

Dzogchen

The highest attainment of the Ningmapa sect that was founded by Padmasambhava is called Dzogchen. This is a system of teaching that provides the knowledge and understanding for discovering our real nature.

In Dzogchen, the teacher uses direct transmission to introduce the knowledge. However, the student has to be prepared through oral transmission, through talks, retreats and the practice of appropriate techniques. Only a qualified and prepared student can benefit from the direct transmission.

I had the opportunity to meet several Ningmapa masters who exuded the type of energy and mind fields that in hindsight had some similarity with Master's transmissions. The most memorable was HH Dudjom Rinpoche, whom I met in a small auditorium in Hong Kong. He was the supreme head of the Ningmapa. Although he only gave a dharma talk for about two hours in Tibetan [there was an

English translator], it was not the substance of his talk that moved me, but the heightened consciousness that I entered into around him.

The Tibetan word Dzogchen is derived from the Sanskrit Maha-Shanti or great peace - a perfected state of Being. It is the realization of the potentiality and power of our real nature. The state of knowing is called rigpa and the normal state of unknowing is called ma-rigma or ignorance.

The distinctiveness of this tantric system is that it teaches moving beyond the static state of Shunyata or emptiness into the dynamic working with the experience of Shunya in daily life. This teaching is about real contemplation that means being in our real condition. This includes emptiness as well as movement.

The vajra is a symbol that is used to illustrate our real condition – samsara and nirvana, that is the absolute versus relative and the pure versus impure vision. The sphere in the middle is our true state and the two ends symbolize samsara and nirvana. There are five prongs going from the middle to each end. The five reaching samsara represent the five elements while the five reaching nirvana represent the five dhyana buddhas.

Since this system was only one of those that I studied and practiced before I met Master, it is not my intention to provide any in-depth pointers into the higher states and cultivation. There are fundamental differences between the views and grounds of Sutra systems and Tantric systems. There are differences between the Tantric systems which rely on transformation and the Dzogchen system which uses the methodology of Self-Liberation.

As an illustration, one can visualize oneself in a mirror. The image in the mirror is not us. However, we have introduced a mirror that is separate from us. In Dzogchen, one would meditate on being the mirror itself and all of images of the world just passing thoughts. This crystal mirror can be a useful tool for realization of our real nature.

A Turning Point

I had already turned twenty-seven years old and after working for over three years, had been promoted to an engineering manager position at the Fairchild Semiconductor plant in Kwun Tong. It was a big responsibility for someone so young and I suddenly had to take over management decisions and deal with hundreds of people issues.

Although my parents were very pleased about my career, I was reaching an existential crisis. I had been practicing my basic Vajrayana sadhana for over six years and felt that I was reaching a block in my progress that would require more advanced techniques. However, in order to get those advanced techniques, I would have to go back to the States and take an eighteen month to three years retreat.

Complicating matters was the constant reminder by my parents that I should settle down and get married. My mom had been trying to find a girl for me for four years but I had a bad reputation with all the matchmakers because I kept turning down all their suggestions. My focus was more and more towards becoming a monk!

One of my main daily meditations was a Guru Yoga of Guru Rinpoche [Padmasambhava] that involved visualizing a complete mandala with the Guru Rinpoche at the center. The practice takes about thirty to forty-five minutes and I would do it at night-time due to my work schedule.

One night, after I had almost completed the meditation, my concentration on Guru Rinpoche wavered and the image changed into distinctly more Indian features and had a turban and beard and I heard a voice in my mind that said, 'Get Married'. I was bemused and thought maybe I had dozed off and had a dream sequence and just ignored it.

To my dismay, over the course of the next few weeks, this disturbance in my meditation occurred a number of times and I was quite discouraged. In order to get some clarity, I wrote a detailed letter to my meditation mentor for advice. After waiting two weeks, I got a response and he counselled me that this may be an answer to my next step on the path. Keep in mind that in the Nyinmapa tradition, it is not necessary for the Lamas to be celibate or be monks, although they do keep long periods of celibacy during yearlong retreats especially in their youth.

After struggling for a few more weeks, I woke up one morning and seemed very clear in mind that my spiritual path in this lifetime was to be a householder and that I had tried being a monk in more than one past life already.

Casting aside any doubts, I informed my mom that I wished to get married. She was shocked but immediately went out to find the matchmaker that was still willing to talk to her because of my younger brothers. She took the bus and met a friend and they started talking. It turned out that this friend's daughter had recently returned from India and she was also wanting to find a match for her. One thing led to another, and they actually didn't need to go to the matchmaker at all, but decided to get together for dinner with both families and let the two of us meet.

The long and short of it was that I got engaged to a strong and beautiful lady. We dated for about six months and then got married.

Now, if that was all there was to it, then I may not be recounting this in a book about my Master. The most amazing fact was that twelve years after I was married, I met my Master, SatGurunath and it jogged my memory because the face that had morphed from Padmasambhava was exactly this yogi!

The miracle of my Master reaching out twelve years before we met and affecting my life in such a dramatic way is a profound mystery to me, but I thank him for his grace and blessing because otherwise, I would probably not have met him in this lifetime.

Figure 13a
A Mandala of
Guru Rinpoche

Figure 13b
My vision during
practice of
Guru Yoga

Figure 13c
Master at Pema Osel Ling
with image of
Padmasambhava

Rudra Shivananda

The Path of the Householder

> As the lotus flower grows in mud yet is not muddied
> As the Hamsa swan separates milk from water
> As royal Janak is not tempted amid his palace finery
> As an enlightened master writes large but leaves no tracks
> May we live a spiritual life in this material world of maya

There is a large divergence in the spiritual path when one chooses to be a householder, living a spiritual life in a material world to fulfill the associated duties and obligations, versus pursuing a monastic life dedicated to spirituality and spurning all worldly concerns. Once I had decided to get married, everything became different.

Instead of deciding something based on my own desires and wishes, I now had to take into consideration my partner's needs. It was not possible to shut myself up during the weekend and focus on meditation if she wanted to go out, which naturally she would since we were both working on the weekdays when we first got married. I would have to get up early but not too early to meditate so as to not disturb her. Of course, this became much easier after we met Master and she also started to practice Kriya Yoga (more than ten years after marriage). However, I'm remembering the early days of adjustment to living life with a partner instead of pursuing a solitary lifestyle.

Once we had children, there was an even more enormous adjustment to be made. The kids' needs always had to take precedence – they could not take care of themselves. Taking care of babies and watching them grow can be very rewarding, but the day-to-day work and worries involved can be very tiring. My wife had to quit her job and became a stay-at-home mom. I had hardly any time to meditate for about five to six years, sometimes squeezing in ten minutes here or there. I became proficient in walking meditation and mindful meditation many years before it was a thing in the US.

Keys for Mindfulness in Daily Life

1. Sometimes we need to say 'no' to something beneficial so that we can say 'yes' to something important.
2. Be present fully in the moment – give your full attention to those you are with.
3. Appreciate the small moments that are shared with others – good conversation, good hug, good smile. Also appreciate those sweet moments by yourself – a good read, a good walk or a good deep breath.
4. Let go of worry, as it prevents you from being present and robs you of joy.
5. Let go of anger, as it prevents your from being present by tying you to the past.
6. Stop comparing with others and be contented with what you have.
7. Do your best and let go of the rest. Be present in each step of your action and don't be attached to the results. This is the key to staying happy
8. Pay attention and don't hurry – you'll miss your life
9. Put a little distance between you and the play around you to maintain a mindful perspective.
10. Always take time every day to sit quietly and reflect.

One of the greatest virtues on the path of the householder is the development of selfless love. Normally, the love that is understood in our youth is that of a quid-pro-quo. That is, if I love someone, I expect a reciprocation - she should show her love to me too.

When one side falls out of love, the exchange is broken, leading to a broken heart, lots of anger, and a dissolution of the partnership. Marriage challenges one's ideas about love and leads one to enlarge their heart to accommodate someone else, especially when there is an understanding that the partnership is for life, and we need to live with each other for better or worse.

There is further expansion of the capacity for loving others when we have children. We love them even when they misbehave. We love them when they say they do not love us anymore. We love them when they ignore us. Being a parent is a crucible for distilling purer love.

Of course, on my path, I learned a lot from my partner and children in letting go of impatience and anger as well as an appreciation for the feelings of others. Once I met my Master, I was able to integrate the many facets of spirituality into my daily life much more effectively.

Kriya Yoga teaches that one should make progress and achieve Self-Realization while acting as a householder. This requires not just an outward renunciation of the world, nor the actual retiring to a cave, but an inner renunciation, a non-attachment to the material world. It requires that the kriya initiate skillfully lives and works in the world of impermanence and ultimate illusion, deriving the resources necessary to accomplish the spiritual goal of achieving the experience of reality.

An example often cited by the ancient yogis is that of the lotus plant that grows and flowers in the muddy waste-waters, but is not tainted by its surroundings. It remains pure, while absorbing the nutrients from the water and the sun.

In the Bhagavad-Gita, Lord Krishna counsels that we should offer the fruits of our actions to the Divine. In this way, we do not become enmeshed in the results of our actions and are free to do our best without attachment. To expect a reward from our actions is a material way of thinking, while to act selflessly without expectations is the spiritual way of being. Even when we are being paid for our services, we need not be attached to the money, but can offer it to the Divine, to be used to maintain our spiritual life and to help others.

Now, from a practical perspective, how should a spiritually inclined person act?

Keys to spirirual evolution on the Householder Path

The first key to the spiritual life is to set-up and maintain a regular practice or *sadhana*. Regularity is critical in overcoming inertia and other obstacles to spiritual evolution. A daily practice, preferably once in the morning and once in the evening, no matter how brief, is superior to intermittent efforts performed for hours. This is due to the continual accumulation of negativity that must be overcome before it has the opportunity to take root in the subconscious. Once rooted and supported by existing negative habit patterns, then the effort to eradicate them becomes ten times more difficult.

Even in mundane matters, we have learnt to brush our teeth everyday – waiting every three days and then brushing for half an hour would seem absurd to our sensibilities. There are those who would brush their teeth after every meal to prevent the build-up of plaque. Take this same enthusiasm into your spiritual life. Perform your sadhana regularly and prevent the build-up of negativity and karma.

The second key is to maintain a constant awareness of our spiritual goal. This awareness is often disrupted by our uneven and irregular lifestyle. Therefore, it is necessary to examine one's lifestyle. Take a few moments to note down your daily and weekly activities and examine them. Do you take enough rest, or are you depriving yourself of your health by insufficient sleep? Are you eating healthy food, deriving sufficient life-force or prana to remain energetic and positive? It is paradoxical that taking good care of the material body is a mark of spirituality. This does not mean that one should fall into the trap of compulsive dieting, exercising, or absorption in body beautification procedures, which have become part of our consumer culture. However, a consistent asana or postures practice is highly beneficial for the physical and energy bodies.

A healthy body is necessary for spiritual evolution. It is recorded that the great yogi Siddhartha Gautama mortified his body through excessive fasting and found that he could not make any further progress in his meditation. Finally, he was so weak that he was dying, rather than evolving, and so he crawled to a stream and bathed himself, ate a small meal, rested and continued his meditation, subsequently achieving enlightenment, and becoming the Buddha. He always taught moderation in all things – the middle way.

The third key is to find a balance between spiritual and material activities. How much time do you devote to your spiritual life? It is not necessary to spend all your time or even the majority of your time on spiritual activities. However, examine your material activities and determine their necessity. Doing things with your family is necessary and working is necessary to support oneself and one's family. Is working late and taking work home necessary? Is watching television necessary? What is commonly called entertainment is usually an excuse for stimulating a tired mind. Rest and meditation may be a better remedy. Strike a balance.

The fourth key is to examine the people we associate with - the relationships that we value. This does not mean that one should give up our long-cherished friendships because they do not involve spiritual activities. It is helpful to cultivate friends who share similar spiritual aspirations and who can provide much needed support. There is a tendency among those new to the spiritual path to try to explain their new beliefs and practices or even attempt to convince close friends to join them. This should be done very delicately and not from a missionary perspective. If one finds that they are not receptive, one should stop annoying them. It is never productive to force your beliefs on others. To keep their friendship, you may sometimes need to downplay your spiritual activities. If and when they wish to know more, they will know to ask you. Don't expect understanding and support from even close family members. They fear the unknown and they fear to lose you. Have patience to explain what you are doing – you may have to explain many times, until they see that you are not becoming a fanatic or ignoring them.

The fifth key is to examine one's work. Since most of us spend the majority of our day at work, if its performance is a hindrance to our spiritual values, then we need to consider a change. It is possible to work and have provision for financial sustenance without compromising ourselves or selling our integrity. It is needful to keep in mind the values of truth (satya), non-harming of ourselves and others (ahimsa), and non-stealing (asteya) when examining our work. Another value to keep in mind is our self-actualization – is the work that you are doing utilizing your highest potential? Are you happy in this type of work, or did you stumble or get driven into it? Is this what you want in your life? Consider moving from a high paying but unsatisfying role to a more satisfying position or moving from a dull low-paying job to becoming self-employed.

The possibilities are many, but we need to have confidence in the Divine will. We need to tune in to the Divine and find our *dharma* or right path in this world. When we came into this world, we came with the self-imposed burden of *karma*, but also with the promise of the right path or *dharma* for all of us. By following our *dharma*, we can overcome all our *karma*, and achieve Self-Realization in this life.

Constant awareness of our goal and constant vigilance of our activities will help us steer a spiritual path through the turbulent seas of materiality.

It is a blessing to know what we need and to not be enmeshed in what we want. It is a blessing to be satisfied with what we have and not desire what we do not need.

>As greedy eyes grasp at worldly toys
>
>wisdom's heart laughs at fleeting joys
>
>Bubbles in a stream, stars lost at dawns sight
>
>A flickering lamp, passing rain, lightning flash
>
>Dreams disappear in wisdom's waking light

Figure 16a
Marriage Ceremony

Figure 16b
Using an Apple II from bed in small apt.

Figure 16c
Meditating where I can

Figure 16d
Fatherhood

Figure 16e
Boating with family and friends on the South China Sea

Weekend family outings

Master with my children

Family photo

*Figure 17
Many facets of family Life*

My parents with their grandchildren

Highways, Byways, & Sideways – Diversions on the Path

Western Astrology

Even as a teenager, I was puzzled by the underlying laws of cause and effect. It seems to me that there must be ways of predicting what will happen in a particular cosmic bubble such as a person's life. When I was very small, my mom would take me to a local Kwan Yin temple where she would jostle a bundle of inscribed sticks until one fell out and she would pay some expert to interpret the answer to a question that was troubling her. On other occasions, she would randomly pick some passage in the Guru Granth Sahib and try to use that as a guide to take certain actions. There were even a few times when I was six or seven years old that, to treat a troubling skin problem, I was taken to a medium whose face would change and start peaking in an altered voice.

This all seemed rather arbitrary and reactive to me. I wanted a "scientific" divination method. In a magazine at the library, I saw an advertisement for a correspondence course in astrology that promised that I would have more control and better understanding of my life path, whether in regard to education, profession, or family life.

After looking up more information about astrology, it seemed promising for the kind of knowledge that I was seeking. I scrounged up some money and applied for the course. After a while, I found out that I was enrolled in the UK Astrology Association's Faculty of Astrological Studies. The material that was periodically mailed to me was from a famous astrologer named Margaret Hone.

The course gave me a fundamental understanding of astrological signs and how they affect the basic associations of the planetary energies in our solar system. The houses brought in the activities and stages of human life. In a short year or two, I learned a lot about psychology and the interplay of factors that can affect or alter a person's life. It was fascinating but by no means simple. In fact, one would have to juggle many conflicting factors and choose only those that seem to apply in certain situation. How to make better choices depended on the number of charts that you practiced on reading. It took a lot of practice and eventually what seems to be intuition as well.

I had some success in reading my school friends' charts and of course decided that I should be a professional astrologer, even to the point of charging for my services. However, the deeper that I went into this discipline, the more discouraged I got. Reading the birth chart to give an overview of a person's strengths and weaknesses was well and good. Even simple predictions about family life, relationships and finances met with success. But, when it came to precise predictions of events at certain time lines, it seemed like hit or miss.

After a few years, I decided that there were too many unknowns and limitations with astrology and decided to give up taking it as a profession, but decided that there was still scope for further studies and as more of a hobby.

Vedic Astrology

It was when I was in the States for my college studies that I once again got involved with astrology - not the Western variety, but the Indian or Vedic discipline called Jyotish. I was browsing at the Shambala bookstore in Berkeley since, as foreign student, I really had no budget for non-school books, when I heard a bearded Indian gentleman in saffron robes talking to someone about Jyotish. I inserted myself in the conversation and soon became well-acquainted with the Swami who was from Los Angeles. We would meet up whenever he came up to Berkeley and it was from him that I learned the basics of Vedic Astrology.

Jyotish has many more tools than are available to a Western astrologer. For example, interpretation of the basic birth chart is supplemented by the divisional charts – D9 (Navamsha) for marriage, D-10 (Dashamsha) for career or D-20 (Vimshamsha) for spiritual pursuits and religious tendencies. These charts help to drill down and make more accurate predications, but require accurate date and time of birth. Other tools for prediction are the Dasa systems such as Vimshottari Dasa, which divides life into a cycle of a certain number of years and, based on the rulers and sub-rulers of particular cycles, can provide very accurate readings.

One of the main reasons, besides the tools available, that Vedic astrology seems more accurate may also be due to its taking into consideration the precession of the equinoxes, a phenomenon that the earth's rotational axis takes about twenty-six thousand years to make a full cycle in the ecliptic. The consequence is that the astrological zodiac is fixed in the sky in reference to the Earth. For example, Western Astrology assumes that on vernal equinox, the rising sun will always be in the sign of Aries. However, this has not happened in more than two thousand years – for the last two thousand years, the sign had risen in Pisces and is currently transitioning to rise in the sign of Aquarius (hence, the popular 'dawning of the age of Aquarius').

A person who thinks he's Gemini based on Western Astrology, could very well be classified as a Taurus according to Jyotish. You would need to subtract around 24 degrees from your Sun ephemeral reading to get the Vedic sign. This is just one confusion in the whole topic of astrology. Unfortunately, there are many pitfalls and difficulties, and one should be very careful to consult with only very qualified and recommended professionals.

It is not my goal to discuss the merits of this science which has been verified and testified to by ancient seers and yogis for thousands of years. Inept practitioners and prejudiced unscientific "scientists" have brought this noble science to disrepute. However, as Sir Isaac

Newton responded to another member of the Royal Society, when his trust in astrology was denigrated, "Sir, I've studied it, you have not."

My goal is to discuss how this most ancient science can bring light to spiritual seekers and what role it can play. It is not to convince anyone of its efficacy or scientific basis.

As I progressed in my spiritual practices or *sadhana*, there was little time left for other pursuits. Being a householder, family responsibilities had to be assumed. I began to disdain astrology and totally dropped it from my consciousness during my thirties and forties, taking heart and courage from the words of Sri Yukteswar as reported by Yoganandaji, "The deeper the Self-realization of a man, the more he influences the whole universe by his subtle spiritual vibrations, and the less he himself is affected by the phenomenal flux."

In the last few years, as I have observed so many spiritual seekers struggling with their lives and circumstances, I have been moved to help them ease some of their suffering and give guidance on overcoming obstacles, so that they can continue on their paths to self realization.

What can be done through knowledge of one's birth-map or horoscope? Again, Sri Yukteswar tells us, "A child is born on that day and at that hour when the celestial rays are in mathematical harmony with his individual karma. His horoscope is a challenging portrait, revealing his unalterable past and its probable future results. But the natal chart can be rightly interpreted only by man of intuitive wisdom: these are few."

According to the principle of karma (full understanding of this cosmic law is beyond us), it is only necessary to remember that it is the complete record of all our thoughts, words and deeds, as well as the law of cause and effect. Karma is also the mechanism which ensures the proper connection between the two.

The physical body carries its karma in the genetic code – a map of physical potentials and limitations. The energy centers in the energy body are limited by the karma brought into the present life. Finally, the mental body carries the tendencies and mental programs called *samskaras*. Scientists are now unraveling the human genome and can tell if a person has tendencies towards specific diseases.

In a similar fashion, the ancients looked at the skies and unraveled the cosmic star maps. From a person's natal horoscope, it is possible to tell the tendencies towards specific diseases and much more. Energetic, emotional, and mental tendencies are all revealed and when placed against the earthly field of action. Furthermore, the likely occurrences of events can also be forecasted when these tendencies are superimposed on the starry timeline (after all, we measure time by the movement of the sun and moon).

Of course, if it was only given to providing forecasts Indian Astrology would be of little value, for what will happen, will happen and what won't, won't. The glory of Jyotish is that there are remedies provided to offset negative events and promote positive events.

Many different types of remedies have been discovered, from the wearing of gemstones to the ingestion of herbs. The most powerful remedies are the mantras or vibration of power. These remedies can help to offset or deflect the effects of karma. If someone was going to break a leg, he may instead twist it. It is usually impossible to totally deny the power of karma coming to fruition.

 Another use of the Heavenly map is for better understanding of our tendencies – strengths and weakness. This is a great aid in developing the niyama of swadaya or self-study. It is the true Jyotish, to dispel the darkness and ignorance from our minds.

I have been able to give guidance to students on the right type of sadhana or practices that they should pursue according to their dharma. It is possible to see the best cosmic energy or deity to connect with for liberation or the right mantra for transcendence.

We must not let our pride prevent us from taking advantage of such invaluable knowledge: "It is only when a traveler has reached his goal that his is justified in discarding his maps. During the journey, he takes advantage of any convenient short cut."

Sometimes, without having recourse to a horoscope, it is also possible to provide similar spiritual guidance from "seeing" the causal body of the spiritual seeker. It is my experience that when this has been done and then later compared with the results from the horoscope, there are remarkable concurrences. However, it is better to make use of astrology since a horoscope can provide a roadmap that the spiritual aspirant can learn from at later periods and throughout their life.

A cautionary note is in order: karma cannot be denied – we must reap the fruits of our actions. What is possible is to channel and fashion the flow of the karmic retribution in less harmful ways. This is a delicate balancing act and generally will require effort from the person involved to take an active role, rather than a passive role.

Gemology and Jewelry-making

> A sapphire in the rough to shine
> Cut, facet, polish, brilliance reveal
> Soul mired in mayic mud unreal
> Burn karma, enlightenment unveil

During my work career, there was a period of a dozen years that I worked for American companies at their overseas subsidiaries, primarily those in Hong Kong. Although stationed overseas, I would frequently have to visit their headquarters in the Bay Area. During my visits, I would naturally seek out the spiritual bookstores to further my spiritual studies.

In one of my visits in the early mid-1980s, I went to a metaphysical bookstore in San Jose and after browsing and picking up a few interesting books, I came upon a large collection of semi-precious stones and discovered that there was a great interest in their use for healing and spiritual attunement. I felt quite drawn to them and picked some up to feel their vibration. Something clicked within me and I decided to bring some back home with me.

In the next few years, I became completely immersed in the study of gemstones and their uses. It so happens that Hong Kong was one of the major jewelry capitals of the world and I had access to rough and finished gemstones galore at very reasonable prices. Never to do things superficially, I enrolled in a gem and jewelry school and soon discovered the joys of lapidary and the techniques of silver and goldsmithing.

Lapidary is the discipline of cutting and faceting gemstones. I found the process of taking a rough stone and crafting it into a brilliant gemstone a sort of spiritual experience. It also seemed to me to be an allegory of the spiritual path, the diamond in the rough seeker becoming a brilliant Self-Realized yogi through the discipline of spiritual practice. I become so proficient that, after I graduated, I was invited to teach lapidary and gemology classes in the school.

During my lapidary experience, I discovered that it was necessary to learn a lot about the characteristics of the gemstones in order to bring out the best from a particular gem. This led me to pursue the study of gemology, which is actually a professional discipline. In order to challenge myself, I took the rigorous professional examination offered by the Gemological Association of Great Britain. It was amazingly difficult with both theoretical papers and a practical examination to determine one's proficiency. Thankfully, I passed and became an accredited gemologist, a Fellow of the Gemology Association [FGA], the counterpart to the USA designation of GIA.

There were some amusing incidents because of my hobby. One of these was an invitation to appear on a British documentary that had one episode about the famous Jade Market in Hong Kong. I was videotaped giving a tour of the market and offering tips on jade buying. This was quite amusing since, although I had made a study of jade, I was by no means an expert in the marketplace and the main reason that I was chosen was because my knowledgeable Chinese friends did not feel comfortable speaking English.

Another interesting experience was appearing on an early-morning show at the local Cantonese television station. I was interviewed several times on different gemstones such as aquamarine and emerald. This was amusing because I had to answer the questions in Cantonese.

In time, my interest in gemstones and astrology found a convergence because Jyotish used gemstones as one of the remedies for karmic issues in the astrological chart. The color, quality and size of the gemstones play an important part when used in this manner.

For example, blue sapphire is concerned with the planet Saturn and so it is used when there is a need to augment the power of that planet or soothe some negative aspects. However, most people would be counselled not to wear a blue sapphire unless their chart says to do so because the negative aspects of the planet can be strengthened and bring about unwanted results.

As an aside, although I had such great interest in gemstones, I seldom wore any on my hand, preferring to wear gold or platinum bands. When I was younger, my mother had me wear jade pendants.

Interestingly, soon after I met my Master, I had occasion to ask him what gemstone I should wear and he told me to get a yellow sapphire that needed to be over two carats. Naturally, I followed his instruction and dutifully wore it for more than ten years. I had the gemstone set in a gold-wire frame with a prong setting. During a trip to Russia to teach Kriya, I had to spend about eight hours in the lounge at the Frankfurt airport. After a blurry sleep and the flight to Eketerinburg, I disembarked and was picked up by one of the students. As we were driving away, he asked me why I was wearing a ring without any gemstone on it. Sure enough, I looked at my hand and found that the prongs had been pulled apart and the gemstone was gone. It seems my karma with that particular stone was over.

Reiki or the Usui System of Healing

After a long period of time overseas, I had finally come back to the Bay Area to live with my family. It was a time of adjustment. It was also an exciting time. There were lots of spiritual and healing movements floating around - a real smorgasbord of extraordinary teachings from ascension, angelic invocations, pyramid power, and so on and so forth.

One healing system that resonated with me was Reiki. This was a system that originated in the 1850s in Japan from the work of Dr. Mikao Usui, an eclectic spiritualist who traveled and absorbed much from the monasteries in Japan and perhaps in China. He reputedly had miraculous healing powers. However, the popularization of Reiki came about by the efforts of Mrs. Takata of Hawaii, who taught and empowered twenty-two Reiki Masters before she passed away in 1980.

I saw an advertisement for a Level One Reiki workshop by a teacher who was attuned by one of the twenty-two Grandmasters of Reiki and decided to check it out. Over a few months, I took all three levels and became a Reiki Master myself, although I did not feel like a Master.

The reason that I pursued this discipline to the ultimate level was that during the first workshop, I was able to feel the flow of the energy very easily. We had lots of practice with fellow students. For me, the next level, where we were able to do distance healing was a revolutionary concept and it helped to give me confidence in the reality of "invisible energy".

After I became a 'Master' (Level Three), I also taught a number of workshops and attuned students to the universal healing matrix. It was quite satisfying to help people in this way.

However, I became somewhat dissatisfied when my teacher took us to the local hospitals and tried to provide healing to the desperately ill patients. Even when we grouped our efforts, we could only help alleviate the symptoms for a short period of time and there were no miraculous healings like those that reportedly occurred when the early Reiki Masters such as Dr. Usui performed their healing. To me it seemed that somewhere along the line, there was some missing techniques or factors.

Later, after I met my Master, he explained the finer points of healing and I understood the need for self-healing and the role that karma plays in every instance of sickness and healing. Since sickness came about through the patients past actions, then the most effective healing is the present action of the patient. This is why yogic healers would prescribe herbs for temporary effects and then give mantras or some kind action for the patients to perform themselves. The connection between the healing methodology and the sickness may not be directly evident.

Master also passed on his healing practice, which he called Shakti Healing, using the power of Sanskrit mantras to connect with the universal divine Mother energies. There are many levels of matrika or divine Mother energies that can help heal major systems or organs or even particular diseases.

In the above few pages, I've touched upon a few of the major diversions that I spent time one. It is by no means a complete list. Noteworthy among others are several Ascension systems, Archangel Channels, and Holographic Re-patterning. Suffice to say, I sampled widely.

The True Kriya

> Day in, day out, begin at the bottom
> Up and down, Climb the mountain path
> Seeking Divintiy at the peak
> My True-Self I meet

There are many different organizations, yogic schools, and individuals teaching many varieties of practices, all claiming to be guardians of the "true Kriya Yoga." This can be confusing to the sincere seeker.

Is there really a true Kriya Yoga? The good news is that most of those groups are keepers of the flame of Kriya. Even though they may teach different techniques or different varieties of similar techniques, many have legitimate claims through their lineages and the common factors that distinguish Kriya Yoga from other types of yoga.

Why then are there so many varieties? The answer lies in the effectiveness of these techniques to provide Self-Realization. Over the last one hundred and forty years, there have been a number of Yogic Masters who have achieved their spiritual evolution through Kriya Yoga, and they have incorporated, simplified, developed and modified what they had learned to suit the needs of their own disciples. It is important to understand that only Masters may modify what has been passed on down to them.

However, no matter how the Masters have altered Kriya Yoga, there are certain features that will remain constant. What then are these distinguishing marks? It is not necessary to invoke oral tradition to determine these features. They have been plainly given to us in two ancient yogic texts and one more contemporary spiritual classic. The three texts that illuminate Kriya Yoga are: Bhagavad Gita,

Patanjali's Yoga Sutras and Yogananda's Autobiography of a Yogi.

Through the transmission of these texts, it is clear that the following are the distinguishing marks of Kriya Yoga:

1. It originates with Babaji, the mysterious immortal whose presence is whispered throughout the length and breadth of the Himalayas. It is said that Lord Krishna learnt Kriya Yoga from Shiva-Babaji, perhaps circa 3000 BCE. During the dark age of 2400 years between 600 BCE and 1800 CE, only very exceptional sages such the Siddha Patanjali could even learn this yoga. As humanity's consciousness once more became ready, the Light of Kriya initiated blessed Lahiri Mahasaya and once more accelerated the wheel of spiritual evolution. All true Kriya Yoga will claim lineage with Babaji.

2. The control and expansion of life-force energy or prana is an essential part of the practice. Lord Krishna says, "Kriya Yoga is the offering of the outgoing to the incoming breath." Here He is referring not just to the common breath, but to the prana permeating the cosmos and within the human body. Patanjali emphasized that tapas or the building of the inner fire by effort was a mark of Kriya Yoga. Fire is built by rubbing two sticks together and in a similar way, the internal fire is built through the practice of cycling the incoming life-force called prana and the outgoing life-force called apana. This is the prana-apana yagna or internal fire-ceremony. Yogananda has very clearly stated that the kriya pranayama is a natural scientific breath that rejuvenates the body cells and magnetizes the spine - the conduit of spiritual evolution. In a similar vein, he warns us that, "Kriya Yoga has nothing in common with unscientific breathing exercises. Their attempts to forcibly hold breath in the lungs is not only unnatural but decidedly unpleasant."

3. A sense of Devotion is required, because Kriya Yoga

is characterized as an "offering," and techniques done mechanically will not be effective. A science of Self-Realization has as one of its key ingredients a sense of the Divine as the True Self. Patanjali emphasized this alignment with the True Self as Ishvara Pranidhana or surrender to one's true nature. Lord Krishna has given the first steps toward devotion and surrender to the Divine by instructing us to offer all the fruits of our actions, including that of our spiritual practice, at the feet of the Divine. Be a Karma Yogi – work with love for the Lord as a matter of duty without a selfish desire for the fruits or any attachment to the results – practicing nishkama karma yoga is true devotion.

4. Introspection and self-study are keys to higher consciousness and so svadyaya is required. This can include the study of authoritative texts or meeting with sages, but will invariably lead to a course of meditation or dhyana. A sense of awareness is necessary to reach higher consciousness. Awareness passes through various stages – in the beginning it can be humiliating and depressing, as we become more aware of our thoughts, words and deeds; then it progress to joy in the expansion of the soul as it aligns closer to the Divine; finally constant awareness leads to constant bliss.

5. Kriya Yoga is for the spiritual evolution of the householder – this has been made clear to Lahiri Mahasaya by Babaji. Lahiri Baba was himself a householder and had children even after being initiated by his immortal Master. Many of his disciples were family men with jobs and responsibilities. Among them was Shri Yukteswar, who was married, but later became a renunciate Swami after the death of his wife. The confusion concerning the belonging to a religious order and practicing Kriya Yoga was caused by the fact that Yogananda chose to become a renunciate because of his single-minded devotion to the Divine and because of the demands of his mission to spread Kriya Yoga in the West.

Yogananda has become the symbol of Kriya Yoga to many (rightly so, for his many achievements), but his belonging to a Swami order has nothing to do with the practice of Kriya Yoga.

It is up to each person drawn to Babaji and to Kriya Yoga to choose the variety that best suits his or her temperament. Each of us has come to this world with different set of burdens and challenges as well as opportunities. Yogananda is reputed to have said that "many paths lead to the top of the mountain, but once reached, the view is the same."

May your choice of Kriya alternatives light up you life, and may you reach the mountain top expeditiously. As Lord Krishna said to Arjuna, "The path of Self-Realization and the path of ego-ignorance are thought to be the two eternal paths of the world. The latter leads to rebirth while the former to liberation. Knowing these two paths, O Arjuna, a yogi is not bewildered in any way. Therefore, be steadfast in yoga at all times."

The Practitioner

Plow the field
Pull the weeds and
Remove hidden roots
Sow the seeds that will
Bear the wish-fulfilling fruits

Abandoning opinions
Letting go of virtue
Passing through knowledge
Seeking truth
Abiding in boundless peace

Part 2

The Practitioner

My Master

Maya the mortal binds
Only a play the yogi finds
Death's claws sunk in mortal hearts
Immortal soma transformed by siddha arts

No holy institution for liberation
No dogma cage to bind nor fancy stage to pray
No ochre robes nor color strobes for meditation
No ego balm so in child's play do not stray

A thousand lifetimes of tears
My soul cry finally He hears
In darkness a light, Yogiraj appears
Liberating me from countless fears

True yogi needs no external tools
True yogi one's body the only school
True Guru the only guiding light
Ignorant ego forces to fight

Shiva-Shakti unparallel gift
Great Seal kundalini to lift
Five-pointed star to light the way
Cosmic hum leads home to stay

Sat-Gurunath Supreme
Wakes me from my dream
Drops drip from nectar well
Saves soul in karmic hell

Soul suffused bliss swell in third-eye sight
In the sky pouring life Surya Divine Light
On Earth Gurunath warrior's might
In my heart Babaji guiding light

Breathing through my breath
Thinking through my thoughts
In thy light I become aware
Thy grace saves me from karmic snare

Clear light of no mind
How rare to find!
Poetical verses I have none
Siddhanath you are my Sun.

Spiritual Practice with a SatGuru

I travelled to many countries and cities, discovering new food, monuments, museums or historical landmarks. It was very exciting, but no matter how much research I did on my own, it was too easy to miss some of the essential food or sights or be unable to reach them because of distance or lack of transport. After a lot of wasted effort, I discovered the joy of local guides who can provide the missing link to immerse oneself in the local culture and experience what they can offer.

On one trip, I was on a big ship entering a harbor, but we had to stop for about thirty minutes outside the entrance. Later, I found out that we had to wait for the local expert to come aboard and pilot us in. There are many such examples in the material world and we do not question the need for professors, teachers, guides, financial consultants and all manner of experts. However, I frequently encounter the question of whether we need a spiritual teacher or guide. It seems strange for such a hesitation when you apply common sense and our everyday experience. Is achieving Self-Realization easier than getting a degree or qualification in some mundane subject?

Receiving a spiritual practice from an authorized spiritual teacher from a specific lineage connects one to all the Masters of that lineage and we get the benefit of their accumulated wisdom as well as direct guidance not only from any living Master but, in rare cases, even from beyond the earthly plane. Still, one's spiritual progress is dependent on one's own effort and discipline in practice. The teacher shows the way and can give guidance and advice.

A much deeper dimension is opened up when one has the blessing to meet a SatGuru who can not only teach, but transform the student by his spiritual power. His Presence can evolve the student beyond the effect of his own practice. It is part of the reason that students are attracted consciously or unconsciously to be around a SatGuru whenever possible and feel regret when separated from his spiritual magnetism.

Master is a SatGuru. In the following pages, I share some of the experiences that he has blessed us with and that I can relate to demonstrate his magnanimity in tirelessly working to evolve humanity's consciousness to a higher level.

Paraphrasing Master's words, he is not a teacher, but a "waker and a shaker".

What is in a name?

For the particular purpose of this book, I've chosen to use the term Master to denote my SatGuru or spiritual master because it is easier to understand. There are two sides to the term from my perspective:

- He is a Master of the Yogic Sciences
- He is the personal Master that disciplines those of us who aspire to be his disciples

Normally, when I talk to him, I would call him Nath which means Lord, or Gurudeva (divine guru). In public or a more formal setting, we would refer to him as Yogiraj. Among his students, we call him Gurunath and when referring to his teachings we prefix it with Siddhanath.

All this might seem rather confusing, but it is actually very straightforward – just as a doctor is called by his professional designation at work but is called Dad by his children and by his first name when he is with his spouse. If he is recognized for some research he's done, the syndrome or cure might bear his last name.

My Master's formal designation is Yogiraj Gurunath Siddhanath. None of these are actually his given or family name. They are spiritual names:

- Yogiraj means the King of Yogis and is a title given by another saint or Master in recognition of a younger yogi's accomplishment in Divine Realization as well as wisdom/proficiency in the teachings and systems of one or more yogas
- Gurunath is a title conferred on the Master of the Nath Yogic tradition. It denotes proficiency in awakening the kundalini of disciples. We also sometimes call him SatGurunath to acknowledge that he is a SatGuru
- Siddhanath is a title conferred on a spiritual Master who has command of siddhis or spiritual powers that apparently defy mundane experience

These titles are not given in an academic environment and may only be bestowed in a one-to-one setting by someone of a senior and revered level, such as one's revered Guru or a living saint.

However, sometimes, spiritual titles are conferred in a more formal setting by spiritual establishments such as when he was given the title of Yoga-Martand (Sun of Yoga), it was in a public ceremony and with much pomp and circumstance.

However, all titles and names notwithstanding, the real test of a Master is his spiritual power to take his students across the ocean of mayic suffering.

Practice - Abhyasa

A pivotal aspect of the spiritual path is one's committment to practice what has been given by the Master. The following is advice on setting up a firm foundation for practice.

Five Verses On Spiritual Practice

Master holds the great avatar (a divine incarnation), spiritual reformer and teacher, Adi-Shankaracharya in the highest regards. This being is closely related to Shiva-Goraksha-Babaji and wrote voluminous commentaries and treatises but when asked to give the core essence for spiritual seekers on the path of jnana yoga, he composed five verses called the "The Essence of Spiritual Practice in Five Verses" :

> Study the scriptures diligently
> Perform well the rituals and actions as described in the scriptures
> Worship God through the performance of ritual
> Keep the mind from desire-originated actions
> Let your sins be destroyed
> Let the seeker inquire into the defects of re-incarnation
> Make a firm resolve to attain to the True Self
> Leave your own home immediately
> *Verse 1*

The first verse is the preparatory phase – the phase of the worldly person engaged in activity who is making an effort to learn more about spirituality. One should refer to reliable and time-tested works of wisdom to engage in the study of the self – this should be done regularly to overcome the resistance of our materialistic tendencies. In the days of the Shankaracharya, it was customary for each person to perform his or her own rituals of worship rather than go to a priest and every youth was taught the proper methods and mantras for this purpose. We are advised not to utilize the rituals for the sake of material gain or for pleasure, but for the sake of removing our negativities so that we can move forward towards liberation from karma. A meditation that the acharya recommends is to recollect the pain and suffering involved with re-birth driven by the wheel of karma. Once sufficient positive tendencies and good habits have been cultivated, and a distaste for cycle of birth and death, then one is ready to make the resolution to seek Self-Realization. The advice to leave one's home should be understood from the perspective of the time when it was necessary to journey great distances to find a Master who could guide the seeker towards the final goal and also the need for staying at an ashram for extended periods of time in order to gain the wisdom necessary. At the present time, it may not be necessary to go to such an extreme as with the communication age, everything seems to be within reach. Spiritual teachers travel all over the world and there are workshops and retreats galore. However, it is good to keep in mind the level of dedication that the acharya is advocating and examine our own use of time and resources. Certainly, a re-alignment even for the householder is necessary as a serious spiritual practice requires a minimum of several hours per day!

> Seek the company of the wise in satsang
> Develop firm devotion to Brahman
> Develop virtuous qualities mental tranquility and restraint of senses
> Let him renounce all rituals
> Let him approach a wise sage
> Let him serve the sage
> Then let him inquire about the indestructible Brahman
> Let him hear the mahavakyas – the essence of the Vedas

Verse 2

Once we have started on the spiritual journey in earnest, then one should cultivate the company of the spiritual Masters and try to listen to them whenever possible – even watching videos or listening to CDs are acceptable. One should now drop all rituals or worship and focus on devotion to the one Divine with meditation on the vastness and orderliness of the universe and by singing praises of the Eternal Now (wothout form or attributes). The acharya recommends simultaneously the cultivation of virtues such as non-violence, truthfulness, non-stealing etc., in order to qualify for becoming a spiritual disciple. It is necessary to make a search for a sage – one who has attained to the state of Self-Realization – the search should include common-sense research to ensure one is not taken in by someone who is either deluded or making a pretense of their level of perfection. Once one has decided on the Master and prepared one self appropriately, one can then approach such a Master with humility and an attitude of service. In olden days, the seeker would be required to stay at the ashram from one to three years taking care of the place and looking after the needs of the Master, during which time he will be tested time and again to ensure that he is ready for the higher teachings. Nowadays, the service would be more fundraising or organization-oriented and will be defined by the Master. When the Master indicates that the seeker is ready, then the seeker becomes a disciple and will be given the appropriate guidance and direction whether by the imparting of wisdom or the bestowal of a spiritual practice, depending on the type of path that is chosen.

> Now, reflect on the essence of the mahavakyas
> from the Upanishads only
> Stop all unnecessary discussions or speculations and
> focus only on revealed wisdom
> Remain absorbed in the attitude of "I am Brahman"
> Renounce feelings of pride and arrogance
> Give up the identification with the body
> Give up argumentation with the sages

Verse 3

The second verse ended with the spiritual aspirant established as the student of a sage and learning at the feet of his Master. When he has learned all that can be learned from the teachings of his preceptor, then it is time for the student to reflect on what has been transmitted. This would typically be the great sayings of the philosophical treatises called the Upanishads which have been sanctioned by generations of sages and shown to lead to the experience of the divine union with one's true Self. The great sayings are called mahavakyas – an example is "Aham Brahmasmi" or "God and I, me and God, are one."

There is a tendency for the student to get side-tracked into other philosophical debates or speculations which are not central to his realization, and this must be avoided in order not to waste time and resources. One should remain steadfast in one's contemplation.

All the mahavakyas and indeed all the Upanishads are meant to lead to the realization that the soul is spirit and that spirit and God are one. To achieve this realization, it is necessary to make an adjustment in our attitudes towards one another and towards the world. We cannot act in a manner inconsistent with this teaching and so we cannot act selfishly or in an ordinary manner, but would have to "love one's neighbor as one-Self."

When one has an attitude of being united with the divine, there is a tendency to be touched by pride and arrogance, however subtly, and this has to be avoided and consciously renounced.

The cause of suffering is our disunity from our true nature and subsequent identification with the body. This physical nature is all that we can know with our five senses and so we have grown to think that it is all there is to reality and therefore we must be our physical body. Together with the right attitude of identifying with the divine is the giving up of the wrong attitude of thinking we are the body.

Once we are established in the right attitude and renounced erroneous ones, we begin to achieve the actual experience of the unity that we have previously only intellectually understood. As we start to glimpse reality, there is a tendency to start sharing with others the truths that we are now convinced that we know. This can lead to confusion and subtle errors, because only when we are fully established in wisdom do we realize that reality cannot be discussed or argued upon as it is beyond our normal consciousness and language. Reality is neither dual or non-dual or combination of both. In higher consciousness, we can experience reality as it is but when we come down to the relative world, where something either exists or not exists, all concepts fail to adequately describe it and so there can be no end to dispute. The normal mind is not equipped to deal with reality - only with a four-dimensional space-time splice of reality. Shankaracharya therefore counsels against arguing with sages.

In the first verse, the acharya counseled the seeker on achieving a steady resolve towards the spiritual path, followed in the second verse with seeking the sage to hear his wisdom. In the third verse, the student needs to reflect on what has been transmitted and acquire his own discriminative awareness.

In the fourth verse, the great teacher examines how the spiritual practitioner should live the material life.

> Practice moderation in food
> Fasting can heal diseases
> Live contentedly upon whatever comes to you as
> a blessing from the divine
> Endure all the pairs of opposites: heat and cold, and the like.
> Avoid wasteful talks.
> Practice equanimity
> Desire not the kindness of others

Obviously, one must support oneself or one's family in a suitable manner, but should not run after excessive requirements, living in contentment with what has been allotted by the universal grace. Practicing moderation in food and fasting at least one day every week builds self-control as well as keeps the practitioner in good health. It is easy to become concerned about one's comfort which can lead to igniting desires for what is liked and aversion to what is not liked. It is important to seek balance in life which can be upset by keeping company with those who are seeking material goals. If the practitioner seeks help from others, it puts one in debt to those who offer support and this must be repaid sooner or later, enmeshing one in the material cycle of action and reaction. Of course, if someone offers unsolicited help, it is not necessary to reject it. In all activities, the practitioner's goal is to stay calm and centered.

In the fifth and last verse, the practitioner's spiritual progress is examined.

> In solitude live joyously.
> Quieten your mind in the Supreme Lord.
> Realize and see the All-pervading Self everywhere.
> Recognize that the finite Universe is a projection of the Self
> Conquer the effects of the deeds done in earlier lives
> by the present right action
> Through wisdom become detached from future actions.

The sage is now united and abides in his true Self, ever in bliss irrespective of the circumstances, and being ever mindful of the Divine. This is an internal state of super-consciousness which is attained during deep Samadhi meditation. The next step is to extend the internal realization to dealing with the apparently external world which is accomplished through first seeing that one's true Self pervades everything, and the apparent diversity is united in the Self – we are all One. In the next stage, the whole of the universe is seen as only a manifestation of the Self and without a separate existence.

In this divine consciousness state, all past karma is wiped clean as if it never existed and the sage now acts only in the present without ego or karma.

Although these five verses are directly connected with the practice of Kriya Yoga, I've found them inspirational and instructional in cultivating a proper mindset for practice. Even with an injunction to leave home and go into solitude, one can think of that in connection with an inner silence and an inner attitude of renunciation rather than with the outward show.

Nothing Seems To Happen?

Too often I hear from sincere seekers that they are trying their best and putting in persistent effort, but nothing seems to be happening with their meditation. It gets very boring, and they are tempted to give up. Doubts arise that maybe the meditation is not right for them or maybe they are not right for the meditation. What's up with this? Shouldn't there be a way to know what's happening with one's meditation?

It is critical to remember that no matter what form of meditation we are doing, the goal is to remove the obstacles that have accumulated in our mental, emotional, energetic and physical bodies that prevent us from experiencing our true blissful nature. In the physical body, our nervous system has been wired from birth with stressful obstructions which need to be cleared away before we can regain our center. It is the same with our mental and emotional bodies. It is the reason that we seem to be overcome by mental and emotional blockages.

Remember that the practices of yoga are for cleansing the karmic blockages and so you know they are working when the thoughts and emotions arise during your meditation! These are the indications that something is being released. Unfortunately, we get hung up with what is being released and oftentimes, we try to fixate on that rather than maintaining our calm during this cleansing process. When you clean house, you don't keep the garbage that is the result, and so you should not keep back the thoughts and emotions which are released during the meditation – they need to be let go of.

We are so used to projecting our minds outward that when we try to focus inward, we get confused and don't understand what is going on. Instead of practicing, we start thinking about what we should be experiencing. One must understand that the mind is continuously in motion. When one is awake, the mind acts as a sensory computer monitoring the five inputs of sight, sound, taste, smell and touch and when one is asleep, the mind takes the memories and re-organizes them to provide dreams. Only when one reaches the state of dreamless sleep does one get a rest from the mind. In the same way, only after the cleansing of karmic blockages is achieved does the mind become restful and the soul can experience its natural Spirit nature.

Accept what is happening during meditation and try not to judge or expect something different – it is what it is. It is what is now. A lot is happening during your meditation. When one says that nothing is happening, it means that what is happening is not what we expect should be happening – this is a mental trap that keeps us from our happiness. When a lot of thoughts come, it is progress and when very little or no thoughts come, it is also progress.

Relax and let the process unfold. Persevere in your practice and eventually, you will experience the bliss of your true Self.

Perseverance In Practice

The spiritual path is long and arduous and has many pitfalls and obstacles. We are often befuddled by our delusions and fall prey to illusions, thinking a true path is false or that we have achieved something when we have not.

Why does this happen? It is because of our karmic tendencies or samskaras operating in our field of experience including the very spiritual practices which are meant to burn them away. We cannot rely on our senses or our minds. We can only trust our heart and the spiritual guide. That is why it is useful to have a trusted guide on the path lest we fall by the wayside.

Once you've done your due diligence to select the guide and the path, the key to success is perseverance. Many have died and lived and died without achieving their true self because of doubts and the lack of intensity in their practice. Many have delayed their realization by prematurely giving up their daily practice. Do not join their ranks.

Practice, practice, and practice more.

It is important to set your priorities – what do you want from this life? Something that you cannot take with you into the next life or something that can endure death? Besides one's karma, the only thing that survives death is spiritual practice. All the great sages have assured us that not one second of spiritual practice will be forgotten and that the fruits of our practice will last for eternity if need be.

You have nothing to lose and everything to gain or, if you want to be very precise, you will lose everything and gain nothing, for only by giving up the impermanent things of life can you gain the immortality of the true Self, which is nothing as it is not an object but you, Yourself.

It is perseverance that moves you to get up early in the morning from the warmth of your bed and complete your spiritual practice before going to work. It is perseverance that keeps you going even when everyone around you may be telling you that it's a waste of time and effort. It is perseverance that overcomes your despair, desperation, boredom, restlessness, and doubt.

Set your sight on the priceless Divine and persevere in your practice, no matter the winds of emotional turmoil or the tsunami of physical and mental distress that come and go.

Perseverence

At daybreak let the sunshine in
Harness will, Breathe prana within
Let love, light and joy begin

At dusk dark let moonbeams in
Control mind, suffuse nectar within
Let bliss and immortal life begin

First USA Retreats with Master – Breitenbush

Master offers several Life and Livingness Retreats every year in North America. These are between three to five days long so that he can give deeper teachings and more advanced techniques to the sincere participants. Some of the most memorable spiritual experiences that I will be relating later in the book occurred in some of these retreats.

Our first two extended yoga retreats were in Oregon at the Breitenbush Hot Springs Retreat and Conference Center in 1995 and 1996. These were great opportunities to spend over a week with Master and be immersed in his presence and practice for extended periods of time.

Every day, Master would lead us at dawn and at sunset to practice our Surya Yoga. Even though we were there in late June and early July, mornings and evenings were cold, but we warmed up pretty quickly. Sometimes, the sun would be hidden in the clouds, but we noticed that in some uncanny manner, it would always peep out just when Master started to intone his salutation mantra to the Sun and hide again when we finish our practice. Master was able to instill in us an abiding connection and trust in the power and grace of the ruling spirit of our solar system.

In these two retreats, we were able to spend invaluable hours practicing basic and advanced Kriyas with Master. It was at this time that he formally initiated us into the techniques that will in the future enable us to perform a higher degree of proficiency in an important aspect of Kriya called Kechari Mudra. Some of the students had been asking Master for several years to give it to them, but he had waited until the time was right.

In both years, we shared the dining facilities with another spiritual group that practiced Buddhist meditation. An amusing sidenote was that we would be talking at mealtimes while this other group had to observe silence. I observed that even though Master was talking, his mind was silent, while those who were outwardly in silence seemed to be wrestling with tremendously disturbing mind-talk to such a degree that it was visible on their faces.

In between meditation sessions, Master would take us for long nature walks and also to swim in fast flowing rivers or in the frigid pools. Master is a great swimmer and loves to meditate in shallow water. There was a large pool that we would dive into that was quite cold in the daytime, but would be freezing in the evening.

One evening, while we had just overcome the initial surge of adrenaline and shivering from slipping into the pool and starting to feel some warmth, we heard a shrill laugh and saw a dark shadow on the path. He kept walking by and waved at Master – I could just make out eyes like flames, but thought it must have been some optical illusion. When we finally left the pool, Master called us over and said that we should call it the Devil's Pool from now on. We laughed because we thought that it was due to a few of the students starting to turn blue and had the early stages of hypothermia, but he explained that the being that walked by was a rakshasa, a devilish being.

The benefits that we received from spending time with Master cannot be described in terms of sensational experiences, but more in terms of the transformation that we could feel in our energetic, emotional and mental dimensions. It is through self-observation that we realize the great work being done for us.

Figure 18a
Hamsas at the Camp
with Master

Figure 18b
A special initiation
session
with Master

Figure 18c
A group photo at Breitenbush

Figure 18d
Swimming at Devil's Pool

Arriving Home – Visiting Master's Ashram

It was not until 2001 that I had the good fortune to visit Master's Ashram, nestled in the foothills of the historic Sinhagad Fort in the spiritual valley of SitaMai, near Pune. The pressures of work and the inability to take sufficient time off had prevented me from going and the years of yearning had built up my expectations to a high degree. The actual experience surpassed my dreams not because of the spectacular visions or spiritual breakthroughs, but by the simple relaxation of my tensions and the opening of my heart to the realization that I had found my spiritual home on earth.

It was a very bumpy ride on the barely graded dirt road full of potholes from the nearby village to the Ashram. After crossing a gulley, we had arrived and got out to take our shoes off so that we could walk barefoot inside. Master had told us that this was very healing even though all we could feel was the brambles and stones scoring our tender soles. All of it was of no concern because of the otherworldly feeling and the heightened effect on my consciousness as entered.

At that time, there were very few structures or facilities. A few of us stayed in a small grass thatched hut opposite to the shrine where Master had his underground meditation cave. There was a kitchen connected to the room where a few ladies could stay – this extension actually had the luxury of a bathroom. Most of the cooking was actually done on the ground outside the kitchen where GuruMaa (Master's wife) and some of her helpers from the village would sit and use an open fire. There was a small, covered rotunda called the Mandala that we could sit inside for Master's satsangs and meditation. Halfway to a hill at the back was a ramshackle set of partitioned rooms that formed a dormitory for four or five people. There were also a few students who were using sleeping bags. As you walked up the hill, you find a small temple with a Shivalinga.

[The Ashram has changed and increased in size over the years. Every time I visited since, significant changes have occurred and now it can comfortably accommodate 100 people. There is also the Earth Peace Temple with its Mercury Shivalinga.]

Master had wanted us to come at this particular time because he was going to have a special celebration at the Ashram, one that was connected to spiritual awakening. It is called Mahashivaratri and is an occasion once a year to honor the Divine Lord of Yoga to receive his blessings for Self-Realization. It occurs on the night before the new moon and is the darkest night of the month of Phalguna, usually in February or March.

We were in great anticipation on the auspicious day and Master regaled us with stories and shared his wisdom all day long. We abstained from food for the most part. At midnight, he led us up the hill to the temple and we sat on the hillside while he performed the Abhishek on the Shivalinga. We then meditated for a little while and followed him down the hill to the mandala, where we chanted and meditated until dawn.

A special ritual of the celebration was the drinking of a herbal mixture that had coconut and baang. The drink helped to put us into altered states of consciousness. My own experience was one of being separated from my body and a profound awareness that I was not that ephemeral body that will be discarded at the end of this particular life's journey.

We spent a week at the Ashram deepening our Kriya practice with Master's grace. Everyday he would take us for a walk during certain times. We particularly enjoyed the visits to the shrine at SitaMai – one of the legendary places that Lord Rama and his retinue rested at on their journey back to Ayodhya after the defeat of Ravana in Lanka, seven thousand years ago.

A departure from the Ashram is always accompanied by a desire to return, and I've had the good karma to return every year since then for the celebration until 2021. Every visit has helped me to overcome karmic limitations and grow spiritually. It was fortunate that I was able to visit in February of 2020 because we were not yet aware of the pandemic that would soon wreck all travelling plans. Even during the last year, Master has further enhanced the Ashram and I hope to visit again soon.

Pilgrimage to the Himalayas

One of the reasons that Master had given me the Adesh (divine command) to come to the Ashram in 2001 was that, after the Mahashivaratri celebration, he was going to lead a small group of students to the Himalayas, retracing the steps of his early days there as documented in the Wings to Freedom film.

During this trip, we had the opportunity to meditate in some of the secret and sacred locations. It was a wonderful opportunity.

Our first stop from Delhi was in Hardwar. We got in rather late, around 9 pm, but Master still wanted to take us to visit a Nath compound. When we found it, all the doors had been locked and it looked like everyone had closed for the day. However, our insistent pounding on the doors drew out a few people who opened up for us and led us to a hall where there were paintings and a counter under which they brought out all sorts of Nath-based mementos.

After we had shopped our fill, Master asked to see the Mahant (spiritual leader) who opened up a gate and led us into a mandir that led down to a secluded cave-like area which exuded spiritual energy. We all sat down and meditated. I felt myself transported outside of my body and flying out into space, merging and emerging from light. I had the feeling that Mahavatar Babaji was all around me. I was pulled back into my body by the sound of Om and Master announced that we should leave. It was one of the most memorable meditations that I had experienced up to that time.

We then went on to Rishkesh, Rudraprayag, Guptakashi, Ukhimat and Chopta. It is not my intention to recount all the amazing experiences that we had at these places because it is better to find out for yourself, if possible. I've had the blessing to visit these places and others since that time with Master and each time was magical. I left with the feeling of having received bountiful spiritual benefits.

Master had a unique way to remove our blockages when we ascended to the snow level at Chopta - he initiated a snow fight among the students! It was exhilarating and we all felt some heaviness lifting from our souls. It has now become a tradition that every year there would be a snow fight at Chopta.

Ukhimat is an otherworldly place. I feel that we would enter another dimension and time whenever we visit. It is a place hallowed by tradition. It was here where five thousand years ago, Lord Krishna came to officiate at the wedding of his grandson. It is here that the relics of Kedarnath are relocated, and pujas performed during the winter months when it becomes otherwise inaccessible. Kedarnath is one of the twelve jyotirlingas or holiest temples dedicated to Lord Shiva.

The Omkareshwar Temple at Ukhimat is so old that part of it is sunken into the surroundings. The space inside is barely enough for half a dozen people to sit comfortably. The core part is many thousands of years old, but it has been restored and rebuilt over time. It is one of the wonders of India that confound Western archeologists who are used to dealing with dead and ancient cultures who have left behind abandoned structures. Since it is still a living civilization, structures are continuously being lived in and worshipped at for thousands of years, one layer on top of another. Take, for example the holy city of Banares which existed as Kashi and Varanasi – it was ancient even in the time of the Lord Buddha.

Another wonder of rural India is the state of transportation at that time. On the way down from Chopta, we discovered that our bus had no brakes, and we were careening down the narrow mountain road overlooking seven thousand feet down the slopes. Some people become frantic but Master encouraged us to do some spiritual chants while the driver used his gears and perhaps his feet to take us back to Ukhimat where we waited for a replacement bus. Miraculously, we found out that the replacement bus also had brake problems but the motor technician who came with it was able to jury-rig something to safely take us to Rishikesh. Please be re-assured that in the last twenty years, the roads have been improved and the tourist buses that are now hired are in very good shape.

> Find heaven on earth
> Spirit within body-temple
> Realize true-Self in self
> Divinity within humanity

Figure 19a
Listening to Master

Figure 19b
Hamsa resting in open bed

Figure 19c
GuruMaa: traditional cooking with village ladies

Figure 19d
Feeding children during Mahashivarati celebration

Figure 19e
Inside hut at the Ashram

*Figure 20a
At DevaPrayag
during Pilgrimage*

*Figure 20b
At RudraPrayag*

*Figure 20c
Master initiating snow fight*

*Figure 20d
Inside tea shop at
Gauri Kund*

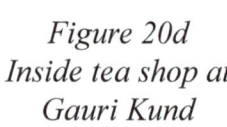

Rudra Shivananda

Spiritual experiences during Pilgrimages

Palani – Lord Muruga

A very sacred pilgrimage site in South India is the temple complex of Palani in Tamil Nadu. This temple is dedicated to Lord Muruga. In popular mythology, Lord Muruga is the second son of Lord Shiva, the lord of yoga. He has many names. In Northern India, he is known as Kartikeya, the leader of the heavenly armies. In central India, he is known as Subrahmanaya. Other names associated with him are Skanda and Kumara.

Lord Muruga is always depicted as an ever-youthful being whose mount is a peacock and who carries a long spear as his weapon. From a spiritual perspective, the peacock is a symbol of the fully opened lotus wheels of life-force energy, the chakras, in the vital body while the spear is a symbol of the awakened kundalini energy in the central spine. I've always been fascinated by the depiction of Lord Muruga, who seems to me to be the epitome of an awakened yogi as well as a warrior-saint.

I was fortunate to be visiting Palani during the major festival of Thai-Pussam. On the bus journey to the town, we saw many pilgrims on foot and was told that many had been walking for up to a hundred miles. It was inspiring to see some of them, who were doing grand prostrations all the way.

We stayed in Palani for a few days and, every day, would go up to the temple. I wore only a dhoti (a traditional unstitched lower garment for men) and walked everywhere barefoot. Below the temple were shops that sold many religious items, the most fascinating were those made from solidified mercury, especially the mercury shivalingas. They gave off a powerful energy, but I decided not to get any because Master had not at that time indicated that we could utilize such items safely. I was traveling on my own and did not have occasion to consult with him until much later.

During the festival, many devotees showed their zeal by piercing their bodies with long needles and carrying weights at the ends. There were others, both men and women who would roll incessantly around on the bare ground. There were those who whipped their backs. Yet others would form circles and have teaching and storytelling. Many chanted, sang, and danced and, of course, there were processions.

In spite of all the distractions, I managed to spend a lot of time up in the temple. We walked up many steps barefoot on one side of the hill and down the steps on the other side. Walking down was always an exercise in concentration because there were many lepers laying around. It was a sad reminder of those in society who are less fortunate.

On the first day that I went up to the temple, I walked around and looked at the statuaries and carvings – there were depictions of the major siddhars or perfected yogis. Then, I participated in one of the daily pujas – the murti (sacred statue) of Lord Muruga was originally made with nine poisonous materials that alchemically gave off healing properties. It was installed long ago by the great siddhar Boganathar.

It was a nice puja, but I was not particularly affected by its power and so decided to sit in a quiet area (it was amazing that I was able to find such a spot in the otherwise noisy environment) and meditated. Shortly afterwards, I felt myself leave my body and expanded upward and outward. I saw an image of Lord Muruga in golden aura superimposed with an image of Mahavatar Babaji. There was the roaring of ocean and a conch being sounded, and then I fell back down into my body.

The experience left me convinced that there was a close relationship between Babaji and Lord Muruga, which made sense since they are both depicted as eternal youths of sixteen summers. Later, during some research, I found that Shiva-Goraksha-Babaji had been Sanatana Kumar and that Sanatana Kumar was also traditionally said to be an appearance of Lord Skanda. My connection with Lord Muruga was very much deepened, as was my connection with the Siddhars.

Chidambaram - Tirumoolar

Another of the famous spiritual places that one can visit is the temple complex of Chidambaram in the southern state of Tamil Nadu. The temple is dedicated to Lord Shiva. It is unique in that the holy of holies in this temple is actually empty and represents ether (the Space attribute) or, to a higher degree, the formless aspect of the Divine.

Of course, the Divine Form aspect at Chidambaram is also very famous – it is the Nataraja – the Dancing Shiva. Many images of this form is available to view on the internet, but the original was setup in this mandir.

After suitable donations were made, we were taken into the inner sanctum and were able to participate in one of the famous pujas. These are spiritual rituals that can remove obstacles on the path and provide benefits depending on the type of energy and deities invoked.

Another highlight in this complex was an area that from ancient times had been the meditation spaces for great yogis called Siddhas or Perfected Ones. We were able to sit in the same meditation alcoves and practice to our hearts content. The most famous of these Siddhas who spent a long time there was Tirumoolar, who also wrote the yogic classic Tirumundiram.

The story associated with this great Siddha is that he was yogi in the Himalayas, called Sundarnath, who was sent by Lord Shiva to spread yoga in Southern India. While he was there, he passed by an area where he saw some desolate cows wandering around and discovered the dead body of the cowherd. Taking pity on the cows, he entered the dead body and rose up to take the cows home to safety. However, when he returned, he found that his original body had disappeared and understood that the Lord wanted him to use this local cowherd's body to spread the teachings of yoga. The cowherd's name was Moolar and as his fame increased, he became known as Tirumoolar, meaning the holy Moolar. His magna opus, the Tirumandiram is one of the twelve sacred scriptures in South India.

Figure 21
Lord Murugan at Palani

Figure 22a
With a pujari at Palani

Figure 22b
Pictorial of Boganath installing the murti of Lord Murugu

Figure 22c
Image of a Siddha in Palani

Figure 23b
At Chopta in the Himalayas

Figure 23a
At Chidambaram

Figure 23c
At Kalimath
Temple

Ekalinga-ji – Lakulisha

After several weeks of traveling down from the pink palaces of Jaipur and sightseeing all the way, we finally arrived in the southern Rajasthani city of Udaipur, a stronghold of the Mewar royal line and famous for its heroic figure, Maharana Pratap Singh.

Master had mentioned to me several unique spiritual places to visit during my Rajasthan trip and one of them was the one thousand three hundred years old temple complex of Shri Eklingji just outside of Udaipur. It is dedicated to Lord Shiva and the central shrine is a five-faced Shiva-Linga made of black stone.

When we reached there and entered, a young man approached and told us that he was an official tourist guide and fluent in English and would be able to take us to the most important parts complex and we would get more blessings than just wandering around. I felt good about this person and hired him immediately. He started by giving an history of the temple and its connection to the Maharajah of Udaipur and pointed out the various important shrines.

Finally, he helped us participate in a puja in the sanctum sanctorum where several priests chanted mantras and made offerings to the Shiva-Linga. We were able to drink some of the blessed and energized prasad. I felt myself entering a heightened consciousness. As we exited, the guide asked how we had heard about this temple, and I told him about our Nath Master and about the Kriya Yoga of Mahavatar Shiva-Goraksha-Babaji. He was stunned that we were connected to the Nath tradition of Gorakshanath.

As we were preparing to leave, he stopped us and said that he had something special to show us and that this was a secret shrine that usually only the presiding royal family had access to, but he felt that we had a karmic relationship with it. Naturally, I agreed.

He took us to a back building and up some stairs and then unlocked a door and ushered us in. As we entered, I felt a stillness enter my very soul and looked at the covered shrine on a pedestal. We sat in front of it, and he removed the covering to reveal a murti that resembled a small pillar with five similar standing figures carved around it.

He explained that this was a murti of an ancient yogic deity called Lakulisha. This was amazing to me because my Master had often mentioned 'The Lakulisha of the Lilac Lagoon' in his talks and when I asked him about it, he would smile and say that it was another manifestation of Mahavatar Babaji.

My mind went blank, and I felt a strong transmission from Master. I immediately started my Kriya pranayama and had a blissful meditation for about thirty minutes, when the guide coughed loudly and apologized that it was time to leave.

Guari Kund – Gorakhnath Temple

One of our favorite places that we visited while on an Himalayan Pilgrimage was Gauri Kund, which is the mythic holy site of the location where Divine Mother Parvati, the shakti of Lord Shiva, had come down for her bath, to wash off the incense and other offerings that had accumulated from the worship of countless devotees.

There is an outside bathing pool that is available for pilgrims to partake of the holy water from the mountain streams. However, since we had come during the winter season, it was technically closed, but we had made arrangement for them to open up the water-spouts to fill up the pool when we get there.

I had been there several times before in past years and so this time I decide to walk around the village that surrounded the Kund instead of standing around waiting for the water to fill up. Almost all the shops were closed down, although one enterprising tea shop opened and the owner smiled and offered me a cup of hot chai. As I walked further, I was drawn towards an alley for some reason and decided to explore it. I discovered that the alley ended at a sort of cliff that overlooked a fast-flowing river but what caught my eye was that across from me was a small open shrine that was connected by an outcropping that formed a bridge across the river.

Curious, I walked across but was stopped by a locked gate. I looked up at the sign that had been erected on top of the gate and saw that it read Gorakhnath Mandir. This was astonishing to me that a shrine to the Immortal Babaji was actually there unbeknownst to us and in such an secluded area. I peered through the metal gate and saw that there was a raised concrete platform and an area around it that people could sit and meditate or listen to a discourse.

The only sound was that of the river flowing underneath. It was quite idyllic. I tried the gate again, but it was padlocked and wouldn't budge. I turned away in resignation and crossed back across the bridge when all of a sudden, a six- or seven-year old girl ran outside and smiled at me. She beckoned and then proceed to cross the bridge. I watched as she held out some keys and unlocked the gate. I returned and opened the gate. Just when I turned around to thank her and give her some donation, I found that she had disappeared. I called out but there was no answer.

It was a puzzle, but I quickly put that aside as I went in to pay homage to the shrine by sitting down and starting to quickly do my Kriya practice. After about an hour, I was deeply immersed in my spiritual consciousness and had a vision of the smiling face of my Master. I smiled back.

About five minutes later, I heard the sound of someone opening the gate and opened my eyes to see Master entering with all the students who had finished their dip in the pool.

I stood up and greeted him. He immediately bowed to the shrine and then proceeded to get a towel and started to clean the platform and remove the branches and other detritus that had accumulated. He then asked everyone to sit and meditate.

Even when we left some time later, there was no sign of the girl or anyone else. I began to feel that this was a blessing from Divine Mother. Master often said that it is easier to pray to the Mother in order to approach the presence of Lord Shiva and so I had been practicing a Divine Mother mantra given by Master for many years.

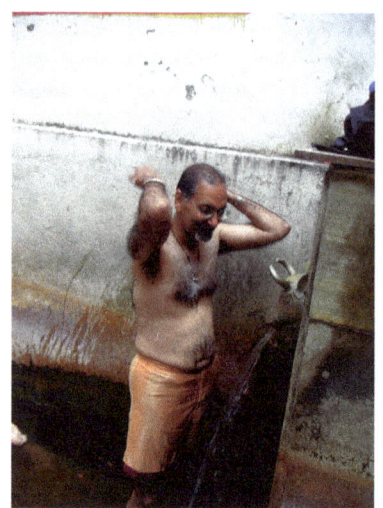

Figure 24a
At Gauri Kund

Figure 24b
At Gorakhnath Shrine

Figure 24c
Gorakhnath Shrine at Gauri Kund

Figure 24d
A side-view of the Gorakhnath Shrine

Master's Revelations

The Master disappears into sunlight

A few years after I had met Master, we had an opportunity to host him in our home in the SF Bay Area for an extended period of time. Living and serving an enlightened being day in and day out is a great purifying and humbling experience. I was blessed with many such opportunities over the years and continue to be grateful beyond words.

On most weekdays, I would be off to work early in the morning and it fell to my late wife Neelu's shoulders to take care of Master's needs. However, on the weekends, I was able to spend more time with him.

One such weekend morning, I had prepared some tea for him and invited him to sit and enjoy it. While he was sipping the tea, his back was to the window and the sun was shining and forming a halo around him. It was getting quite surreal, and I was feeling the effect of his energy transmission in my heart center.

Smiling, he remarked that he had previously written a poem about "A cup of tea" and he started to recite it in a melodic cadence, transporting me into a otherworldly sensation.

To my astonished eyes, he gradually merged with the sunlight and disappeared. I could still hear him and vaguely see a shadowy outline when I squinted but he had become insubstantial. I was lost for words and only managed to keep a blissful smile on my face. I felt that Master had almost let go of some sort of anchor to the material world, and was reminded that he often told us that 'matter is only congealed light'. This was a realization of that truth.

The Master disappears into a Black Hole

Oftentimes, while staying in the US, Master would visit the homes of some of his students to encourage and bless them. During the earlier years, I was the designated driver and would accompany him during such visits.

One time, while he visited a couple in San Jose and after he had been served his dinner, he sat on a sofa with a cup of tea and started to talk about spiritual matters - a mini satsang. I sat about five feet to the side from him on the floor and was absorbed in what he was explaining.

After a few more minutes, I found that he was literally becoming darker and darker and seemed to be absorbed into a Black Hole – I could even see some little lights around him like stars that seemed to be blinking out. Even after closing my eyes for a few seconds and re-opening them, he was still there only in presence. A few more blinks later, he came back to normal.

This was quite a shocking phenomenon, and I didn't say anything until we were in the car and driving home. He smiled and said that he was in a still-mind state even though he was talking and that in such a state, it is possible to draw in all the light like a celestial black hole.

It was confusing, but there was no doubt that something had happened, and it was not hypnotism or some sort of hypnotic suggestion since he didn't say anything beforehand or during the experience. Subsequently, Master demonstrated this same phenomenon during his Satsangs and many people have experienced it as well.

**Master had tea with me
Dawn's sunshine behind
Mystic ode,
a rhythmic light
Sparkling sight,
Can this be?
Motes of light,
Master's might.**

*Figure 25a
Master disappears
into Light*

*Figure 25b
Master
disappears into
a Black Hole*

He Comes From the Stars

Master has a great affinity with nature and would always take us walking in the forests in a sort of walking meditation. In other times, he would take us to meditate immersed in or besides water, whether it was the ocean, a river, or a lake. He would also take us oftentimes to look up at the stars on a clear night. Of course, during the morning, he would work with us to connect with the spirit of the boss of our solar system, the Sun. Master taught us by his words and actions that the Divine is not only within us but all around us.

During one of our many Life and Livingness Retreats at the Mt. Madonna Center, I had a direct vision of the mystic nature of Master. Nestled in the forests that cover the Santa Cruz Mountains, this center provided us with a spiritual environment for the deeper work that is the blessing of spending a few days in his Presence.

One night, after a satsang and meditation, he announced that we would meet outside for a walk. It was around 11pm and so we needed to get our flashlights and outdoor clothing and met outside the hall. He then took us walking down a paved path and cut through into the forest. We had to spread out as the forest paths were very narrow and in some cases non-existent. We would have to follow him as we jumped across fallen logs or undergrowth without falling or twisting our ankles. We had to be very aware of ourselves and the surroundings.

He took us walking for about forty-five minutes and we had to double back a few times as we lost sight of the track. Finally, he led us out of the trees and onto one of the main roads that led back up to the building where we were staying. It was past midnight, but everyone was still energized. As we slowly gathered around him, he looked up at the sky. It was a clear night, and many stars were present as well as visible planets, notably Jupiter.

I was turning around and craning my neck up to view the panoply of stars when I felt myself standing apart and entering a meditative state. A constellation jumped out into my consciousness, and I somehow realized that it was the constellation Orion. In the space above the belt, I saw an image approaching and it was a majestic version of Master, growing clearer and bigger until he merged into another star outside that I thought was Sirius. By that time, I had come back to my senses and looked around to see Master looking pensively up at the sky.

It was clear to me that Master was a Divine Spirit that had come down at the behest of Mahavatar Babaji to help the humanity of this ball of matter called Earth and raise our consciousness. Master had long ago, in ages past ascended to the stars. He has come back from the stars to speed up the evolution of humanity.

Master and Babaji

Master had often talked about his experiences with the Immortal Mahavatar Babaji and what it means to be a direct disciple of the Lightning Standing Still (a term Master uses to describe Babaji). It was all very theoretical until I had a taste of what he meant during a retreat with him at the Headlands Institute.

Headlands in those days was a very primitive center - almost like an army barracks - but the ambience was wild and natural and Master loved the big waves and the strong winds. We arranged retreats there for several years.

This particular morning, after an awe-inspiring satsang, he was guiding us in a meditation when, all of a sudden, he interrupted himself and strangely said that he had something to do and that we should close our eyes and practice our Kriya for a little while.

As far as I know, everyone else closed their eyes and started their practice, but I kept my eyes open because recently, I had started to practice with my eyes open, especially in his presence. My motivation for this was that I wanted to experience a higher consciousness while engaged in everyday life and felt that practicing with eyes open would be a beginning for that level of awareness.

Almost immediately, I saw the amazing vision of Babaji flash in a bright light from Master. I blinked and he was gone, replaced by a tremendous painfully bright light all around him. I closed my eyes and opened them to find that the light was still there. It was a very different light from that which surrounds him and spreads outward to us when he gives us the Shivapat experience of his samadhi consciousness. This was painful and seemed too much for me whereas that usual experience was gentle and re-assuring.

I realized that I had been privileged to witness a very special relationship between Master and Babaji. It felt like Babaji had come through Master and was using his physical presence for some special purpose in the world.

Jai Nath! Jai Babaji!

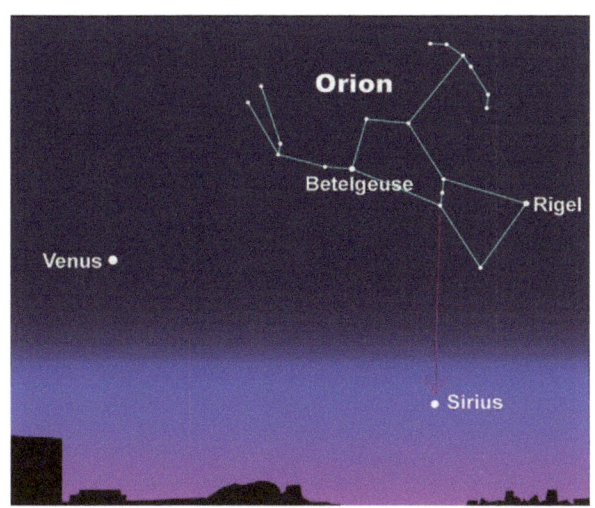

Figure 26
Experrience of Master and the Stars

Figure 27
Master and Shiva-Gorakhsa-Babaji

Rudra Shivananda

Master on Healing

There have a many miraculous testimonials about how Master has been able to directly heal those who have sought his help. I can only talk about what I have seen or experienced. An important caveat is that due to his family's entreaties, he no longer gives overt healing but everyone who comes in his Presence can benefit from the natural healing that he transmits constantly.

I myself have not had occasion to avail of Master's physical healing, but can testify to his powerful energetic, emotional, and mental healing power. Sometimes, this can occur in an innocuous and subtle manner. There was one time at the Ashram when I seemed to be under a lot of energetic stress and seemed to be weighed down with blockages. I saw him walk near. It was the first time that day and, as was the custom, I went over and bowed to make pranam to touch the ground near his feet. He walked closer and my head wound up bumping into his stomach. We both laughed and he blessed me and walked off. Right after my head bumped into him, I felt a shift - a lifting of some great burden - and the blockages that had been bothering me since my morning sadhana disappeared.

During a satsang in San Francisco, I saw a woman entreat Master to heal her son who was suffering from life-threatening ulcers. He used his hand to pull out the ulcers and then blew them away. The lady later let us know that her son's ulcers had almost disappeared according to their doctor. Unfortunately, I then learned that Master had taken on the ulcers into his own body and although he eventually healed them, he suffered the pains for some time. It was then that he instructed us on the karmic consequences of forcefully healing that which might not be meant to be healed.

One time, I was in a car with him and a Hamsa (a member of Master's spiritual movement) called for advice on something, and during the conversation, mentioned that she was suffering from a migraine headache. Master casually said that he would pull the headache out for her and did it, even though we were in different cities.

Another time, a lady devotee from Hawaii called up to our house while Master was visiting and wanted to talk to him. I naturally inquired about the why of it and she confided that she wanted to check if he was really there because that morning, her husband had an operation which went well and afterwards, he told her that Master had been there during the operation. He saw him before he went under the anesthetic and knew that he would be fine.

Master taught some of us certain healing techniques which he called Shakti Healing which invokes the power of the Universal Divine Mother. It has hands-on as well as distance healing modalities, but my understanding from him is that the True Healer is the Divine and the best healing is Self-Healing. He stopped teaching the healing techniques because he told us that most of the students did not practice enough Kriya to be able to do healing – one should practice four hours of Kriya to be able to give one hour of healing.

Master Manifests in the Sun and the Moon

Those of us who have followed Master for a while have been blessed on many occasions when he would use the energy and power of the Sun or the Moon to heal or transform us.

Many years ago, in the late 1990s, on a full moon night, we had congregated with him on the beach at Santa Cruz. He taught us a whirling full moon meditation, after which we laid down on the sandy beach for a few minutes.

He then asked us to stand up and face the moon and told us that he was going to use the healing light of the moon to help overcome any bothersome emotional problems. We were to think about what we wanted to get rid of, then look at the moon, breathe in the light of the moon, and then expel forcefully the negativity. We did that for a few minutes and then closed our eyes.

Afterwards, we walked along the beach for a while. A few of us started talking together and we all simultaneously blurted out that we had clearly seen Master's face smiling at us from the moon during the whole time. We started asking the others and almost everyone offered the same experience.

It was quite common for us to practice the Surya Yoga (the solar healing practice that Master developed and which we will talk more about in Part 3 of this book) with Master at dawn and sunset, especially during retreats.

One time, it was dawn and we had walked with him to a nearby beach. He asked us to look at the rising sun and we all clearly saw his face blazing from it. Are these our imagination at work or are there experiences that transcend our rational minds? What we consider impossible or miraculous routinely happen around Master and so many of us are unfazed when such events occur. Human nature is such a strange thing!

Figure 28a
Master Manifesting through the Sun

Figure 28b
Master Healing through the Moon

Pilgrimages

Besides the Himalayan Pilgrimages, Master also would sometimes take us to the holy places in South India.

In addition, he also encouraged us to visit certain spiritual sites on our own. It would be difficult for a person to visit all the holy places in India during one lifetime because there are so many and also some are difficult to get to.

The most important for yogic practitioners are the twelve jyotirlingas and the fifty-two Shakti Piths because of their powerful spiritual energies. The jyotirlingas are the most holy and powerful temples dedicated to Lord Shiva while the Shakti Pithas are the sites dedicated to the Divine Mother. Jwala Mukhi would be an example of Shakti Pitha.

Of the twelve jyotirlingas, there are three which are in Maharashtra and relatively easy to reach. They are Bhimashankar near Pune, Tryambakeshwar near Nasik, and Ghrishneswar near Aurangabad and Ellora Caves.

During our visit to Bhimashankar, we had the blessing to participate in a powerful Rudra Abhishek (a benefical puja or spiritual ceremony) in the aura of the Shivalinga in the inner sanctum. It felt very purifying. While walking in the back of the complex, we encountered a small shrine to Gorakhnath and were able to meditate in front of it.

During our visit, there was some construction going on and, while we were walking down some steps, I noticed a long sharp steel pole in a dangerous location that would've poked out my late wife's eye. I was walking a few steps behind her but managed to jump in front of her and blocked her from walking into it. We were both shocked but gave thanks to the Divine grace and Master's protection.

I was initially disappointed when we visited Tryambakeshwar because it was a Monday and there were long lines waiting to go in. It took us over two hours in line to only have a few moment's darshan of the Shivalinga. After exiting, I wandered around the complex and stood entranced at a trishul that had been affixed on the ground and entered a deep meditative state of higher awareness wherein everything and everybody was surrounded by glowing light.

The Ellora Caves are magnificent, with both Buddhist and Hindu iconography. For me, the highlight was the Shiva Temple carved from a single piece of large rock. We were in the area for a few days. After visiting Grishneswar, we returned to our hotel in Aurangabad and, this time, I noticed a sign for a mandir close by. When asked, the concierge mentioned that it was Matsyendranath Mandir, and this intrigued me. It turned out to be only a five-minute walk in the back through a garden and some trees.

There was a main building and several smaller side structures. There was an open door and light in one of the side structures. Inside, I discovered a life-size murti of Matsyendranath and information about this temple. As I came out, there were a number of people walking by and they told us that they were members of this temple and that their leader had arrived and was going to give a satsang. They were very friendly, and we were invited to the satsang and it was very interesting to learn of their teachings which were also suitable for householders.

The Presence of Gorakhnath

During my trips to holy places, even though my outward goal may be something different, it seems that we as Master's students have a great affinity for stumbling upon temples dedicated to Shiva-

Goraksha-Babaji.

It is not well known but there are literally hundreds, if not thousands, of shrines to Gorakhnath. There are at least twenty temples that I'm aware of just within Maharashtra.

On one trip, we were going down to Kohlapur to visit the Mahalakshmi Temple there. It is a five- or six-hour drive from Pune. When the driver heard that we were of the Nath Lineage, he took us on a side trip to visit two Gorakhnath Mandirs. This is just one example.

While touring the Udaipur Palace in Rajasthan, we came across a large shrine dedicated to him.

In the next section, I have talked about a trip to Himachal Pradesh. The dharamshala that we stayed in belonged to the Nath tradition and had a large Murti of Matsyendranath on a fish. The Divine Mother Temple of Jwala Muhki was established by the Nath yogis and there is a large monastery of Kanphata Nath monks there.

Let me not forget to mention the Gorakhnath temple in Gauri Kund where I was led to it by the kindness of Divine Mother.

Due to our connection to Gorakhnath through Master, I've had spiritually beneficial experiences at all the sites associated with this manifestation of the Immortal Babaji.

Ascent to Jwala Mukhi

It is always fortunate to be able to visit spiritual centers where great Masters have done their tapas or spiritual work for humanity. It is doubly auspicious to be able to make the visit in the presence of a living Master as well. This was the case in 2001 when in I had the opportunity to participate on a pilgrimage with the Master.

One of the key spiritual centers which Master led us to experience with him during the remarkable pilgrimage was Jwalaji, at the site of an ancient extinct volcano. This site is double treasured because it is both a Temple of the Divine Mother, as well as a Temple for Babaji Gorakhnath, the divine immortal.

We reached the sacred site in the early evening and sat down outside the temple where a group of pilgrims had gathered around three devotees who were chanting to the Divine Mother for deliverance from suffering. We joined in as their rhythmic drumming and chanting was very pleasing and soon mesmerizing as well.

Jwalaji is where, in the beginning, the Goddess energy manifested her Vak or Divine Voice in the form of flames. Vak is the essence of the Vedas and is divine wisdom and knowledge. Devotees in constant and reverent procession file past at the appointed times when the temple gates are opened and they can obtain the darshan or divine grace of these living flames which appear in seven niches or crevices around the ancient walls. In spite of all the jostling crowds and the constant noise, it is an incredibly peaceful and centering experience. Great rulers of India have worshipped the Mother at Jwalaji and the current Golden Dome above the temple was an offering from Maharaja Ranjit Singh, the great ruler of Punjab during the early part of the nineteenth century.

Behind and above the Goddess Temple is the edifice of the Gorakhnath Temple. This was built around a small space called the Gorakh Dhibi where, during the years around 1000 AD, Shiva-

Gorakhsha-Babaji spent some time meditating to purify and stabilize the region. There is a community of Kanphata Nath Yogis, some quite young, with large earrings in their split ears. This is done to stimulate certain spiritual nadis or currents in the body. A few of the pilgrims had unique experiences in meeting and talking with these dedicated spiritual practitioners from a common lineage to ours.

Early one morning, I decided to go to the temple at sunrise. We were staying at a hermitage outside the village and while I walked through the deserted streets in the calm of dawn heading towards the hill on which the temple was situated, there was a spring in my step and a steadiness in my heart.

I walked past the deserted and shuttered shops, and just as I reached the incline that began the ascent towards the temple gates, a long-haired and bearded sadhu in flowing robes appeared from the side. He smiled and asked me what I wanted. I replied that I didn't want anything and was just going up early to sit for meditation. He nodded, but once more asked me what I wanted.

From my past experience, itinerant yogis are generally looking to give their blessings and would expect some offering of money in exchange. I reached into my pocket and came up with a five hundred rupee note (a lot of money at that time), but he only shook his head and asked me what I wanted. Rather surprised by his refusal of the money, I looked carefully at him and was struck by his radiant face and unblinking magnetic eyes. As I stared into his eyes, I became a little boy and innocently stammered that I wanted to achieve moksha or liberation. His smile widened and he placed a hand on my head and gave his blessing with, "let it be so!" I was transported to another plane of reality and when I returned to an awareness of my surroundings, he was gone. I marveled at what could still happen in this day and age.

After meditating at the temple, I walked back down and was just in time to meet with a group of pilgrims walking up, surrounding Master. He called me over and told me that I had missed the morning jalebies (a syrupy sweet beloved in Punjab and surrounding states.) However, he said that the sweet shop was making a new batch and led me back to the shop and we sat down and we had the most delicious jalebies imaginable, as well as a cup of hot chai.

Later in that evening, we went up again. The Naths showed due reverence to Master and allowed us greater access to the Temple than they would normally. We were able to examine the large number of paintings describing the stories of Babaji's activities more than a thousand years ago. They showed divine personages and great kings paying homage to the Ancient of Days - another epithet for the immortal Babaji.

Later, we were allowed to sit near the everlasting dhuni or fire-pit of Gorakhnath, and had an unparalleled experience of the Arati, a ceremony of light and sound worship offered twice every day. We vibrated with the raw, primeval, indescribable, and rhythmic beats of the Nath instruments, which together with the chanting opened the chakras or spinal energy centers of all the participants. These percussion pieces looked like they came from the iron age – they were rough and lethal looking weapons rather than musical instruments.

The highlight came as one of the Naths simply brushed aside the ashes covering the dhuni, and the flames leapt up in glory. This dhuni was the yogic fire lit by Babaji and has been active for over a thousand years continuously.

We all thirst for such experiences, but we should be warned not to frivolously try to seek out such experiences without the means to modulate the raw energy, which might disrupt our energy centers beyond our capacities to absorb. That is why normal pilgrims are restricted to stay outside the Arti area and can only indirectly hear the ceremony. The darshan of the flames at the Goddess Temple, on the other hand, can be safely experienced as often as grace manifests.

As if the Arati was not enough, we also had the blessing to be allowed into the small cubicle of the dhibi itself - a small space just enough to fit three or four of us at a time. There we had the darshan (visual experience) of the fire and water, a mysterious manifestation of the kundalini shakti. I will be explaining more about this powerful spiritual energy in a later section in connection with the practice of Kriya Yoga.

Master and Shirdi Sai Baba

During the frequent Shivapat transmissions given by Master during satsangs, besides the stilling of my thoughts, I would almost always see his face flickering and changing rapidly. Some of the recognizable images include Swami Shri Yukteswar, Shirdi Sai Baba and Moses. According to my understanding, these were all incarnations of the same avatar as my Master. Essentially, he was those great beings and many more throughout history and pre-history and somehow, everyone who saw the same images had past-life connections with that manifestation of Master.

On one of my trips to India, I decided to visit Shirdi, the town that had grown because an enigmatic figure called Sai Baba had appeared and taught there. There were many stories and miracles associated with him. I had also watched a movie of his life. Of course, the main reason that I wanted to go was because of the connection with Master.

We spent a few days in a hotel a few minutes outside Shirdi and every morning would go there to meditate. On the first day, we arrived in the evening at the mandir and mixed with the evening crowd to participate in an evening aarti. The guides told us about several spots including an old tree that the saint frequently sat under. We went to the tree and felt a great blessing.

The next morning, we arrived at around 5:30 am to line up and participate in darshan of the murti of Sai Baba during the morning aarti (ceremony of fire and light). Although this was built and setup after the saint's passing, the energy was still palpable, and the bhakti (devotion) was amazing.

Then we went out to the town and a guide introduced us to the various spots in which Sai Baba meditated or performed miracles. There were several places that still retained his presence that helped us get into deeper states of consciousness. One particular spot really affected me greatly and I didn't want to leave, but, after forty-five minutes, reluctantly gave up my spot to someone who was waiting to go in.

All in all, I cannot say that there was a great shift in my level of consciousness as there have been in some other places, but I left with a sense of satisfaction that I had somehow accomplished some past life desire. There was a greater sense of peace. Ironically, from that time, I would see less of Sai Baba's image during the Shivapat experiences.

There is a great mystery in how Sai Baba and Shri Yukteswar both lived at overlapping times and yet were manifestations of the same avatar. According to Master, it is because an avatar can manifest more than one body, called nirmanakaya at any time. It is beyond our current level of understanding.

Figure 29a
Image of Matsyendranath

Figure 29b
Nath Yogi giving a satsang

Figure 29c
Master inside Nath Temple

Figure 29d
Golden Dome of Jwala Mukhi

Figure 29e
Painting of Chimamasta

Figure 29f
Master inside Devi Mandir

Figure 30a
Murti of Gorakhnath

Figure 30b
Master wearing turban

Figure 30c
Altar inside Nath Temple

Figure 30d
Sideview of Altar

Figure 30e
One of the paintings inside

Figure 30f
Outside the Nath Monastery

Rudra Shivananda

Purifying the Heart & Tame the Wild Beasts

We are well aware that our hearts are filled with desires, and they interfere with our practice and the attainment of higher consciousness. It is necessary to purify our hearts of desires before we can make rapid progress with our sadhana.

One of the myriad names of the Divine is the Lord of Beasts – Pashupati - which is usually considered to indicate the Lord of created beings. However, from the internal perspective, wild animals are the internal emotions, uncontrolled desires, and passions which ravage our peace of mind and an important part of attaining higher consciousness is to tame these wild beasts, becoming in a microcosmic sense, a lord of beasts ourselves.

We possess a menagerie, a veritable zoo within our minds – the lions of pride, the wolves of hunger, the boar of lusts, the bison of ignorance, the deer that run in fear, and so on, as far as our imagination can reach. On the other hand, we also are aware of the emblems of domesticated animals such as the bull that attends the Lord or the lambs that came to witness the birth of a Jesus. These tame animals represent our human nature rising above our animal nature.

Higher consciousness is about rising above the animal consciousness to the human consciousness and staying in the human consciousness. This can only happen when the lower wild animal nature is tamed. Moreover, higher consciousness is about rising above even the human consciousness to the level of Divine consciousness – a superhuman feat.

In the first phase, to tame the wild beasts, we need to apply self-control. In our society of excesses and consumerism, self-control is thrown out the window. Popular society encourages a level of letting go of constraint – from over-eating to over-sexing, from over-acquiring to over-emoting. Self-control is confused with repression in pop psychology and discouraged. Accordingly, it is better to let out some steam than control the anger.

In most spiritual traditions, it has always been recognized that controlling one's thoughts, emotions, speech and actions are the first steps in attaining the goal of higher consciousness. In yogic traditions, we have narrowed it down to no more than five areas for self-control:

- Tell the truth and don't lie. This includes living your truth as well – walking the talk, so to speak!

- Refrain from harming other living beings. This includes looking after your own well-being also.

- Refrain from wasting your life's energy on non-essential activities – you can enjoy yourself but not over-indulge.

- Refrain from stealing. This includes taking credit for the work of others.

- Do not be attached to things – all things are transient.

The sages have determined that if we practice these five rules, we can tame the wild animals. For instance, we lie or harm others because of fear or desire to gain something, or because of pride. So, refraining from lying or harming others controls the animal passions of fear, desire and pride. Let us look forward towards celebrating the birth of Christ within each of us. Let us consider the rules of self-control that we may tame our animal nature and eventually have our own Christmas day through our spiritual practice.

Rudra Shivananda

The Foundation of Yoga – Ashtanga

In the Yoga Darshana (Patanjali's Yoga Sutras), an eightfold or ashtanga process is defined, from self-restraint (yama) to unity consciousness (samadhi).

It is instructive for us to understand why the yogic sage Patanjali has placed ahimsa (non-violence) as the first of the yama. Non-violence is the most important practice to perform – it leads to the perfection of love. It is the most practical to practice because it is very easy to observe whether one has broken the self-restraint in action, speech or thought. The perfection of love removes the veil of duality and ignorance, merging into satya or truth – the highest aspect of which is the realization of the essential one-ness of all Being. With the perfection of satya, all covetousness is removed and non-stealing or asteya happens in due course. The ultimate in stealing is the thought of keeping something away from the Divine, the giver and owner of all there is. With the perfection of asteya, all that we have is offered to the Divine, which is what brahmacharya is all about – the turning of all our energies toward the Divine. When we have given our all back to the Source of All, what is there to be attached to anymore? The perfection of brahmacharya leads effortlessly to the practice of aparigraha or non-attachment.

Although the five restraints in the yamas is given as a progression, one leading to the next in perfection, this does not mean that the spiritual seeker needs to wait for the perfection of one before practicing the next. They should all be practiced in unison as a completely integrated way of life. However, each cannot be perfected until the previous one has been perfected first, and therefore ahimsa is the most important one to work towards.

When the yamas are perfected, there is an emergence of saucha or purity, the first of the niyamas (higher virtues). The purpose of the self-restraints is to provide the ground for purity and by perfecting purity, all thoughts, words and deeds become sanctified and will no longer incur new karmic consequences. With the perfection of purity, contentment or santosha arises in consequence. You might now start to wonder how contentment could possibly lead to austerity.

Tapas (austerity) is actually the development of inner fire, and this inner fire requires the quenching of all desires, which can only occur when contentment is perfected. When the inner fire has developed by burning all the desires, it is then possible to realize one's true Self, and svadhyaya (self-discovery) becomes a reality. With the perfection of svadhyaya, one can truly surrender to the will of the Divine and practice the perfection of ishvar pranidhana.

Again, the niyamas are a natural progression from the yamas, and each niyama smoothly merges into the next.

The third anga of Ashtanga Yoga, after niyama, is asana (steady posture) because when one has perfected the niymas, one has control over one's physical body and can achieve a steady posture for deep meditation.

The fourth anga is pranayama, the control and expansion of the life-force energy. This pranayama is a practice of combining the tapas or building of inner fire, done with self-awareness of svadhyaya and with devotion to the Divine, in a state of ishvar pranidhana. By the continuous and prolonged practice of pranayama, the state of pratyahara, the internalization of the senses, comes about. Pratyahara is the consequence of the consistent practice of life-force control.

The deepening of pratyahara leads to dharana or one-pointed concentration, which leads to dhyana or meditative awareness, which leads to samadhi, states of blissful absorption into the Self and eventually the Divine. Each limb of Ashtanga Yoga flowers into the next, as opening blossoms encouraging the growth of the next higher lotus bloom.

From the perspective of understanding the perfection of these eight aspects of Yoga, they are like the steps on a ladder leading from our current state to the yogic state of Self-Realization. You have to go from one step to the next. However, from a practical or constructive model, these eight parts are like the spoke of a wheel, and we need to practice them according to the yogic system that we are engaged in.

Yoga is not possible without the fragrance of the yama and niyama - their purifying and transformative power – they are the foundation of Yoga. Let us firmly make our progress on the spiritual path by building the strong foundation of self-restraint and self-discipline for higher virtues. My own experience has convinced me of their importance. So much so, that I wrote a whole book on this subject.

> Restrain that mischief mind
> That dividing mind, that scheming mind
> Abide in the calm ocean of natural being

Spiritual Awakening

A sign of spiritual awakening that I've found among my fellow spiritual practitioners is the dissatisfaction with popular modes of dealing with the meaning of life and the role of humanity in the universe.

The seeker after higher consciousness examines the acceptable ways presented by society to understand the essence of our existence only to find them wanting is some respect or other. This leads to despair until the path is shown that gladdens the heart and illumines the mind.

There have been and still are three traditional ways in the West that sought to understand reality – the paths of religion, philosophy and science. Those of us who try to hide from the mysteries of life and focus on the forgetfulness of desires and "living our lives," try not to think about these paths except in passing or disinterest. Others have tried some variations of these three paths. Some of us merely flirt with them while others commit themselves to one or the other. However, each one way has its benefits and limitations.

Religion starts with the vision of some great soul who tries to communicate his enlightenment to others in their culture but soon becomes a narrowing and exclusive institution run by unenlightened souls who substitute dogma for spiritual experience. Instead of loving all of humanity, religion becomes sectarian and compartmentalized, with its leaders justifying all manners of atrocities by twisting the words of its founder and inventing some new dogma. The genuine seeker who can find so much good and commonality between the words of the great Masters who have given rise to these religions are mystified and horrified by the actual state of their institutions.

Through philosophy, great souls' endeavor to understand through their minds the great secrets of human existence in this vast universe.

In the past, these seekers after the truth have tried to provide answers to others and satisfy their thirst for meaning in life. They engaged in sincere inquiry and honest debate. Although the great philosophers have not been able to formulate one single model of reality that can satisfy everyone, their attempts have yielded all manners of mental heights. Unfortunately, in the last one hundred years, philosophy has become institutionalized and compartmentalized as well, becoming more and more academic, divorced from the concerns of both religion and science. It has become arid, yielding profuse numbers of lackluster academic papers rather than the fruit of a life-long pursuit of truth. It has become a hobby, a university discipline, or a trivial pursuit having little relevance to how one lives one's life.

The material benefits of science have been quite evident from the technological tools and toys that have made life easier, more comfortable and enjoyable. Science has greatly enhanced our understanding of the physical body as well as the physical aspects of our universe, from sub-atomic particles to black holes. However, it cannot provide any answers for those who wish to understand the spiritual life because science has restricted itself to what can be detected by the five senses or instruments which are the extensions of these senses. Before science will consider the spiritual world, it demands that we provide detectable and measurable proof of its existence. Unfortunately, all of science's instruments and tools have been designed for the material world and are not suited for anything non-material. This is like footballers in a football field trying to tell swimmers to demonstrate their skills in the field. Science can only satisfy those who wish to belief that there is nothing beyond this lifetime and the material world.

Is there another solution for the sincere seeker? We need to consider the ways of the East, especially the Masters of India who have always insisted on an integrated path. Only a way that combines the principles of religious devotion to one's higher Self or Divine nature as the goal with scientific methods of experiencing these higher states of consciousness and the appropriate philosophy to support the mental needs of inquiry is satisfying for us.

True Yoga is such an integration of the higher aspects of religion, philosophy and scientific methodology. Without devotion, yoga becomes mechanical and mentally dry. Without philosophy, the mind will wander and doubt such that the practice cannot be sustained over long periods. Without methodical and proven techniques, one merely engages in wishful thinking or emotional hallucinations.

When a seeker rejects a non-integrated path, it is the beginning of discriminative wisdom and an awakening to higher consciousness.

Stages of Transformation

I've explored some key concepts from Patanjali in previous sections on practice. Some other useful terms such as chitta, vritti, and nirodha can deepen our understanding. A fundamental term used by him is that of parinaama or transformation.

Parinaama is a dynamic process and not a specific state of awareness. It is the process of transformation that when applied to consciousness, leads to the state of Self-Realization. According to Patanjali, parinaama when applied to the modes of matter, such as the five senses and the five elements, will lead to the achievement of siddhis or special powers. In the course of normal activities, parinaama is the change that occurs in all phases of matter, including the accumulation of karmic dispositions called samskaras.

Before we begin discussing the various parinaamas, it is important to point out that these consciousness transformations can only truly occur in the states of samayama and not in normal consciousness.

Keep in mind that the three states of dharana (concentration), dhyana (absorption) and samadhi (ecstatic unity) together constitute what is called samayama. The parinaamas are operating on the stored or seed impressions at a deeper level and not on the gross thoughts which have already been dealt with in earlier stages of meditation.

The first transformation is called nirodha parinaama in which the chitta-vrittis become suppressed by expanding the space between mental impressions. When one seed impression disappears and before the next seed impression appears, there is a momentarily gap of no-mind just as when motion in one direction has to be reversed, the object in motion needs to come to a temporary rest first. The transformation occurs when the no-mind gap is extended. The seed impressions are caused by the karmic samskaras and vasanas – the habit patterns and programs from past lives. By the application of effort, a new samskara is built up which aids in the transformation until the gap of nirodha can be extended at will and indefinitely without much resistance.

The second transformation is called samadhi parinaama. The natural tendency during the first parinaama is for the stored impressions to be highly diverse and so we choose a particular object for samayama and it is the form of the object which leads to more focused and specific streams of impressions. In this transformation, the seed impressions are replaced by the essence of the object stripped of its name and form. The mind is transformed into a consciousness of direct cognition of the object – the mind stuff takes the form of the object repeatedly.

The third transformation is called ekagrata parinaama or single-pointed transformation. This occurs when the subsiding seed impression is the same as the arising seed impression. During this transformation, the gap between the arising and disappearing seed impression is expanded to such a degree that the seed impression itself can disappear as if it has been split apart, leading to the seedless or Asamprajnata Samadhi state or the avastha of nirbija.

Signs of Progress in Pranayama

A primary yogic practice is the use of breath to control the life-force energy and direct it to awaken our potential divinity. A spiritual path such as Kriya Yoga is structured such that most of the practitioner's sadhana is based on the pranayama. This is according to the principle that prana and mind are directly linked and mastering prana leads to mastery of mind and the awakening of higher consciousness. Kriya pranayama merges seamlessly into Dhyana and eventually Samadhi.

All sincere practitioners will experience certain signs during the course of their daily efforts and there always arise questions about whether these are positive or negative. I am relating the main milestones that are common to everyone so that you can feel reassured that there is no cause for concern. However, there may be other symptoms which are specific to certain physiologies and karmic dispositions and cannot be covered in a general.

One of the first effects of pranayama is the occurrence of heat and sweat. This is caused by the purification that is taking place in the physical and subtle bodies and are good signs of progress. The perspiration carries the impurities out with it. Gradually, the perspiration will decrease as the bodies become more purified. If the sweat becomes a distraction, rub it into the body or if there is too much, use a towel to wipe it away before continuing the practice. Sometimes a side-effect of the purification is restlessness which can be addressed with improved posture and mental control.

The navel chakra or manipura is one of the first subtle energy centers to be affected by pranic practice. Sometimes air or gurgling sounds can be present in the digestive system. The primary positive sign is the feeling of heat or light in the navel as the fire element is transformed into a dynamic spiritual power called tejas. The purification of the digestive system is closely related to the transformation of the nervous and endocrine systems.

With the opening of the higher chakras, one starts to experience colored lights and various sounds. Sometimes some sadhaks get confused that the sounds are caused by a physical malady called tinnitus. These pranic sounds are such that when one does not focus internally, the sounds tend to disappear. During certain practices, the sounds can be quite overwhelming but in a positive way. One does not get irritated by them. There is no need to dwell too much on them either as they are like sign-posts on the road – one should keep practicing and not be diverted by thinking of them.

As your pranayama progresses, you may spontaneously enter into blissful states. These can be quite pleasant and there is always the questions whether to stop the practice and follow the bliss. It is generally better to continue the practice. The reason is that these blissful interludes are sporadic and may disappear in a month or a year as different karmic configurations come into play. The regular practice leads to Self-Realization and a continuous blissful state that is not dependent on karma.

I hope this helps to settle some of the questions in the minds of sincere practitioners. Due to the lack of personal guidance, many seekers get confused and stop practicing because they don't know if they are doing something wrong. Spiritual progress can get delayed because of doubts and irregular discipline. Seek out a qualified guide, follow a proven system and don't get diverted by doubts.

Transformation - Stages of Spiritual Practice

When we talk about sadhana or spiritual practice, most often we highlight the techniques and the progress in proficiency of practice. We might give tips on how to practice better or guidelines to overcome certain obstacles that will occur along the path.

However, it may be instructive to examine the psychological stages that a spiritual practitioner will go through once he or she starts on the path, irrespective of the particular path or techniques. It is helpful to put one's practice in perspective and also to understand why we observe certain characteristics or behaviors from someone at certain times.

A dominant characteristic of someone who has recently started a spiritual practice is the need for information from the community or from a teacher/Master. The principle psychological need is for external validation of one's chosen path. The practitioner is in a cocoon of joy when at last established in an evolutionary journey, but still harbor doubts. The mind seeks to alleviate concerns through as much information as possible from the internet, fellow practitioners, books, and teachers to make sure that the techniques are being practiced correctly and remove any doubts about the path. This is a necessary stage but when prolonged, may indicate incompatibility with the particular practice or path.

When the practitioner becomes proficient and established in his or her sadhana, the focus shifts to physical, astral or mental experiences. One becomes engrossed in the visions, dreams, or flashes of intuition that arise in the course of the practice. This is a dangerous phase because it can lead to dependence on experiences that are inconsistent and often non reproducible. When some insights turn out well, one is in ecstasy and feels validated but, when they fail, one is depressed and doubts the effort put into one's practice. It is important to let go of such external experiences in order to make progress.

At the third stage, the practitioner no longer concerns oneself with external experiences or psychic gifts. He or she is joyful in the practice itself and would sooner give up eating or sleeping than miss the daily practice. One knows that the purpose of one's sadhana is spiritual transformation and can observe the changes to one's own thoughts, words and deeds as a result of the transformation. At this stage, the practitioner is truly established and will not be shaken to give up his or her chosen path. All that is required is regularity, perseverance and the divine grace for a long life to finish the path.

Dispassion – Vairagya

Success in spiritual practice requires dispassion. Vairagya or dispassion is detachment from worldly objects and ultimately from the three principles of existence, the gunas. It is our desires and aversions that force us into relationships with objects. We need to recognize that these desires do not reflect our true needs. The desires arise from our false conception of reality, of the self rather than the Self, and its illusive relationship with objects.

All spiritual practitioners must cultivate and perfect dispassion. Yoga is not achieved by the techniques alone. Patanjali in his Yoga Sutras (1.2) has revealed that, "Yoga is the restriction of the fluctuations of consciousness." The modifications of consciousness are the cause of our normal non-realized state and when these fluctuations no longer afflict the consciousness, there is freedom from desires and the consequent suffering.

Further, the great yogi has given the recipe for Yoga in 1.12: "The restriction of the fluctuations is achieved through practice and dispassion." Therefore, vairagya is necessary and has to be cultivated together with one's sadhana or spiritual practice.

There are various methods traditionally used for achieving dispassion. These include:

- Intellectual analysis to dispel the false conception of reality
- Creating a strong desire into which all other desires are subsumed. This is generally achieved by recognition that the only true desire is the desire for God
- Expanding selfish desires into Universal Love

Dispassion can also arise from the repeated experience of samadhi (super-conscious state of bliss) or by a vision of the True Self.

The analysis of desires will lead to a realization that a desire does not equate to a true need. Desires come and go and what seemed very important last week may now seem unnecessary. A desire does not have an absolute value. We can entertain multiple desires at any moment - some are stronger, and some are weaker. Desires are impermanent because they are related to objects and all objects are impermanent.

It takes great effort to satisfy our desires by acquiring objects. There is greater effort expanded to keep and guard them, and finally, one is consumed with regret when one loses them. At any moment, we are beset by multiple desires jostling for our attention and eventually, one of them takes the lead and demands satisfaction. One makes the appropriate effort to satisfy this desire and there is temporary satisfaction and fleeting happiness, followed by another desire coming to the foreground. The new desire leads to a temporary disillusionment with the hard-earned attainment of the previous one, followed by the thought that maybe the new one will give true satisfaction.

In this way, if one can give up one's illusions and see through the disappointments, one can release all the energy locked up with preserving the illusions.

The process is continuous until, by the power of samadhi, even the latent desires in the causal body rises up and can be seen and removed. These desires are dormant and do not normally show themselves but may, when given the right circumstances. A rich person may be honest because he has been taught to be so and has never had any reason to be otherwise. However, only when he loses his money will he discover whether he is truly honest or only suppressing dishonesty.

Let us consider the following parable to help us be free from the bondage of desires:

A young sadhu who had devoted himself to the practice of yoga was visiting a temple and encountered the daughter of a rich merchant. She talked to him for some time about his life and the places he'd been. They fell instantly in love with each other, or at least so believed themselves to be. The desire to be with her was overwhelming and he considered giving up his spiritual practice and returning to the householder ways. She told him where she was staying and asked him to see her next day, as she would be leaving with her father on the journey to return home in a distant part of the country.

In the night the sadhu prayed at the image of Lord Shiva. He prayed to be free of his temptation. However, the desire grew stronger. He started to repeat the Lord's mantra, but his mind was clouded. He fell asleep and when morning came, he made up his mind to join the merchant and win his daughter's hand in marriage.

He became an apprentice in the merchant's business and then, over time, became his most trusted assistant because of his hard work and sharp mind. He then asked for the daughter's hand in marriage and soon had a family and took over the business after the merchant's passing away.

He was happy and contented. Then fate took a turn, and he lost his whole family to a plague. Soon after, in his grief, he began to take interest in the welfare of others, participating in charities. However, due to his neglect, the business suffered, and he lost everything to his unscrupulous partners.

As a beggar he wandered around the pilgrimage sites wondering what his life had been about. He became totally disillusioned and began to teach others about the futility of desires.

One night, the broken old man wandered into a temple and sat in front of the Lord's image. He then discovered that it was the same temple from which he had abandoned his spiritual life. He prayed for forgiveness and fell asleep with tears in his eyes.

Next morning, he awoke and was astonished to discover that he was still a young sadhu and that it had all been a dream. He had lost all desire for the girl and married life. With renewed vigor, he pursued this spiritual path and soon achieved liberation.

The first step towards dispassion is to identify the source and nature of desires and achieve freedom from them.

Non-Attachment

It is taught by the wise that attachment causes unhappiness in life and that the practice of non-attachment is necessary for spiritual development.

We do not frequently examine our attachments nor consider them in a negative light since it is taken for granted that a major goal of life must be to experience pleasure and we are therefore attracted to activities that may satisfy the craving for pleasure. It is through the five senses that we derive most of our pleasures and so we are attached to the sensations from the five senses. The senses depend on the body and mind because the sensory organs are in the body and the mind processes the sensory input to give the experience of pleasure – we are therefore also attached to the body and mind.

When we see someone or something that we are attracted to, we form an attachment to and would like to repeat that experience, so a desire appears in our minds. Desires multiply without limit as we become immersed in the senses. Memories of pleasurable experiences become attached to the desires and our thoughts gravitate towards the gratification of the desires. As we give our desires more and more importance, our thoughts, words and actions rotate around our desires as our earth rotates around the sun.

We can form an attraction to any sensory input from any one or combination of sense organs. We can therefore form a desire from something seen, heard, smelled, touched or tasted. The attraction to a particular type of food might involve the visual aspect, the taste and smell, as well as the texture (touch).

When we are unable to satisfy a desire or our attempts to satisfy a desire is thwarted, the emotion of anger arises. We become angry and strike out at everyone around us. We also become angry with ourselves for the failure to gratify ourselves. Anger becomes an automatic reaction to the inability to satisfy a desire and so we oscillate between desire, satisfaction or pleasure, and anger, sometimes spending much more time and energy in the desire and anger phases then in the actual enjoyment phase.

In fact, sometimes, even during the enjoyment phase, the desire for a repetition of the pleasure might arise already and then the emotion of fear rears its uninvited head. There is fear that the pleasure will not come again and therefore this might be the last time the desire is satisfied, or fear that the pleasure will be less next time around. This forms a complex emotional /mental reaction or habit pattern of desire, pleasure, fear, and anger.

The reaction pattern of desire, pleasure, fear and anger causes stress and unhappiness. The physical, energetic, emotional and mental health of a person suffers from the stress induced by the attraction and attachment. A person becomes free from tension when there are no desires. Stress and tension leads to the tendency towards ill-health as the body and mind are more susceptible to physical, emotion, and mental disease agents.

Desires impact not only us, but can have significant effect on others and may even alter the fortunes of countries and the whole world. Many stories have illustrated the impact of desires. A notable Indian epic, the Ramayana, is replete with examples – the desire of Rama's stepmother to usurp the kingdom for her own offspring led to the untimely death of her husband and untold hardship for the people of the country. The desire of Sita, Rama's wife, for the golden deer led her to send her brother-in-law and protector away, resulting in her being kidnapped by Ravana, the demon-king of Lanka. The desire of Ravana to possess Sita led to a great war, resulting in his own death and the death of countless heroes. Another epic, the Greek Iliad, recounts how the desires of Paris and Helen for each other led to the great Trojan War that lasted for ten years.

On smaller scale, the attachment to form (such as standards of beauty) has led to girls starving themselves or developing eating disorders. The attachment to relationships has led to the suicides of discarded partners. The attachment to one's ideologies has led to terror bombings and other heinous acts.

Desires are a fact of life. What can you do with them? There are at least three ways of dealing with them – one can satisfy them, one can repress them, or one can detach from them. Trying to satisfy our desires is like trying to chop off the head of the mythical monster with many heads – whenever you cut one head off, several appear to take its place. There is not enough time in a lifetime to satisfy all our desires. Repressing our desires only deepens their hold on us. We spend all our time thinking about them, even fantasizing about them, and sooner or later, they will burst forth uncontrollably, causing all sorts of damage. The method recommended by those who have wisdom is to detach from them - to let them pass by without focusing your energy on them. The practice of detachment is extremely difficult but the only one of the three that can lead to happiness and extrication from the cycle of desire, pleasure, fear, and anger.

The practice of detachment is essential for those on the path of spiritual evolution as well as for those who wish to be happy in this life and enjoy good health and long life. One way of detachment is to offer the fruits or results of one's actions to the greater good of humanity, or to the Divine Principle of the Universe - something greater than our ego-selves. In this way, we are not attached to the results, whether pleasurable or painful, and yet be able to enjoy them.

Please do give a little thought to how our attachments are affecting our lives – this will increase our awareness in all our thoughts, words and deeds.

Don't Let Fear Rule You

Fear is an impediment to spiritual practice, just as it is an obstacle to all human accomplishments. Everyone thinks they know all about fear, but few ever think about it, trying to avoid it as much as possible. The fact is that this emotion is so basic that it is almost impossible to become free from it. Fear arises from the instinct of self-preservation which was very important in the early days of humanity. We needed to react to mortal threats with the flight or fight program in those primitive times. However, we are still under the same programming without the same stimuli – there are no saber-tooth tigers hunting us these days. The fear of death is one of the most enduring one, that a human possesses.

It is the lesser variations of fear which dominate in modern times – stress and tension. Fear comes and goes – if you see someone point a gun at you, fear may grip your heart but when he puts the gun away, immediate fear is relieved. However, stress is like background music - it is always there. We have little means to release stress because we are not even aware that it is there because we have become used to it. Paradoxically, only when one has attained complete relaxation does one recognize the encroachment of stress.

We do not require an immediate threat to feel some mode of fear because we have evolved beyond animal consciousness to human consciousness. The blessings of imagination and thinking ahead, which animals do not possess to any degree, have the double-edged consequence of causing stress. When a person thinks about the consequence of his action or inaction, such as being late for work or an important meeting, stress is increased. If you imagine yourself losing your job, more stress will spoil your life, but is it an imminent danger that requires such a reaction? We are doing it from habit and cannot stop.

We have been programmed from infancy to react with fear to certain stimuli. It is the punishment and reward system in the family, school, work, and society that habituates us to fear the results of failure (however that is defined). Even when success is achieved in a certain activity, the process has set up so much stress already that we cannot even enjoy the relief.

Tragically, there is even a fear of the unknown. It creates another level of stress that adds to the fear of death. Imagine a stress cake with many layers – the bottom layer is the fear of death and then additional layers are piled on based on our situation.

There is such an emotional perversion that we seek out "harmless" situations that can excite our imagination with horror and fear. Have we ever wondered why so many people actually go and watch horror movies so that they can get scared? The reason that fears and stress can become so habitual is because there is an adrenaline rush when we get scared – remember the flight or fight instinct that we have from our evolutionary past.

I would contemplate on the various kinds of fears and how they arise and then disappear. Then, meditate on how stress was affecting my life and what it would feel like if I were totally relaxed and unaffected by fears. It was very helpful.

Examine your lifestyle and mark down those activities that are contributing to your stress level. It might be a good idea to change or even omit these activities in the future. Don't think that we can't change things – make the effort now.

Jnana Yoga – Advaita Vedanta

When we practice Kriya Yoga, we are aiming for a state of Self-Realization. What is this state? I found my answer through studying Vedanta.

Before I met Master, my main practice after I became a householder was a combination of mindfulness and Jnana Yoga, the yoga of knowledge. The reason is that it is possible to make progress in both in small chunks of time and at any time of day or night. Also, there is a lot of texts, from the ancient Upanishads to modern treatises by contemporary Swamis that I could find in the bookstores that I frequented. I studied the works of Adi-Shankaracharya without reservation – the most available text that was widely translated being that of The Crest-Jewel of Discrimination.

Even after Master had initiated me into Kriya Yoga, I still would practice Jnana Yoga when I was not immersed in Kriya, because the basic premise of Vedanta is consistent with the underlying philosophy of the Kriya Master lineage.

The basic premise is that only the True Self, the Atman is existent. Atman is God – 'aham brahmasmi' – I am God is the supreme truth. The same consciousness that pervades the universe is the same as that which exists in our Being. Vedanta is the philosophy and practice of Self-Realization.

In Advaita, the creator is not the ultimate reality. That ultimate reality is the Absolute called Brahman, which is beyond all attributes and descriptions. This Brahman transcends time, space and causation. It is also called Paramatman, the Supreme Self. Our individual Self or Atman is one with Paramatman, not just a part of it. The creator arises from Existence, Being, Bliss (Satchidananda) which arises from Paramatman.

Vedantic meditation is a three-step process, First, one 'hears' [reading with attentiveness is also fine] the teaching with a receptive mind or open heart, then one should think hard on it until meditation happens, and finally, meditating until realization occurs. The thinking in step two is with full concentration and intent towards self-understanding. Step three requires consistent self-examination and self-remembering throughout the day.

Until recent times, jnana yoga was mainly the practice of renunciates. With the popularization of the Atma Vichara or Self-enquiry as taught by the twentieth century yogi-saint, Ramana Maharshi, it has become accessible to householders also. The basic theme is "Who Am I?"

Although there is not much in terms of documentation on the process, it is possible to begin with a simple meditation on the subject-object dichotomy, or the seer and the seen. A five step process is recommended:

- Discriminate between seer and external objects – our eyes are not affected by changes in external objects that we see

- Discriminate between seer and sense organs – we are not our eyes. The seer can notice blurriness in the eyes or other imperfections

- Discriminate between seer and mental states - emotions such as anger and fear come and go, but even when they disappear, the seer remains

- Discriminate between seer and ego – the self that identifies with the body, emotions, and mental states is not the seer because the seer can observe the ephemeral states that the ego is attached to

- Abide in the True Self, the seer, the witness, that is free of objectivity, letting go of the mental fluctuations as if they are just bubbles in the sea

We can practice Self Inquiry while sitting in meditation or in the midst of a busy workday by asking the fundamental question, "Who is the doer?" We can practice in nature while sitting beside the ocean or while walking a mountain road. There is no limit.

The Power of Kundalini

The word kundalini can be derived from the word kundala which means "coil" and refers to the symbol of the coiled serpent. Just like a coiled spring, it possesses potential energy ready to be awakened as the spring is unleashed. It is a nuclear power station within each of us, ready to be turned on. However, this might never happen during a lifetime. The presence of kundalini is a recognition of the fact that we are only utilizing a tenth of our mind.

The word kundalini can also be derived from the root kund which means "pit" and refers to the place where the kundalini resides – that is between the first and second chakras in the subtle body, where it lies dormant.

Kundalini is the spark of the cosmic Shakti or divine Creative Matrix (Goddessence) that is present as potential divinity in each human being. When it is awakened, it opens all the energy centers on its path to the crown center where it unites with divine consciousness, gracing one with the state of God-Realization.

This individuated divine power is also described as "serpent power" because it is described often as a small red snake coiled three and half times around a shivalinga, the symbol of divine consciousness and of the universe itself.

There is a fine energy channel running in the center of the subtle spine, overlaying the physical spine. This central energy channel called sushumna nadi runs from the first energy center at the perineum up to the seventh center in the crown. It is closed at the bottom by the head of the serpent kundalini and so is dormant.

The goal of yogic techniques is to awaken the sleeping serpent so that the opening to the sushumna is unblocked. When refined life-force energy flows up the central channel, each energy center in turn "lights up" until the seventh is attained. This is the process of Self-Realization.

The kundalini being an aspect of the Goddessence is both the cause of keeping us in the limited consciousness of ignorance, as well as the liberator form the suffering of life and deliverer into the freedom of super-conscious states. This corresponds with the concept of Maya which is both the power that keeps us enthralled in the illusive nature of relativity and also the power that releases the sincere practitioner into realization of the absolute consciousness of reality.

The symbology of the three coils has many layers of meaning and can be understood to refer to:

- The three gunas or principles governing material manifestation

- The three shaktis of will (ichha), action (kriya) and knowledge (jnana) which are necessary for the formation of name, form and ideation

- The manifestation of Creative Shakti as:
    - Nada – primordial sound or vibration
    - Bindu – the primordial source or point of manifestation
    - Bija – the seed or medium of creation

In some yogic texts, kundalini is said to have eight coils, symbolizing the eight chakras and the eight powers or siddhis of perfections, which arise from the awakening of kundalini.

During the process of physical manifestation, the kundalini moves down from the seventh chakra to the first chakra inside the sushumna nadi and as it rests around the shivalinga, it closes the central channel, obstructing the path to divinity. This is the downward path from spirit to matter.

Only by the sincere practice of Yoga can the sleeping kundalini be awakened, and Self-Realization attained. This is the return journey home – the process of spiritual evolution, back to the Source of All.

There is a contemporary misunderstanding that the arousal of kundalini can be dangerous. The term kundalini psychosis has even been coined to describe the various conditions that are alleged to be caused by misdirected kundalini. It must be made clear that kundalini is intelligent and will not take a wrong route. It will only rise when the conditions are correct and the central channel is purified. So, what is really going on?

These distracting and sometimes debilitating conditions are caused by excessive prana or misdirected prana. When people with damaged energy channels try to practice the powerful spiritual disciplines which require control of life-force energy, there can be negative consequences. Even when such people come near yogis or high energy spots, there can be prana overload. Some people are born with damaged nervous systems or damage their nervous systems by drug usage or even accidents. Damaged nervous systems simultaneously lead to damaged energy systems in the subtle body. It is necessary to repair the damage prior to spiritual practice.

The primary systems of yogic discipline that enable the rising of Kundalini Shakti and her union at the seventh chakra with Divine Consciousness are scientific processes which need experienced guides and should not be learned through books or those who are not qualified to lead practitioners on the path.

Ad-hoc Parenting

Haven't we all wondered why we never had to take parenting classes before we become a parent? Being a spiritual practitioner does not necessarily lead one to be a better parent.

My own parents were still teenagers when they married and I came along. They did their best and I'm very grateful for their love and care. However, their were lots of bumps along the way, especially when I went against my Father's religious upbringing.

When I became a father, I was just as clueless. However, I did know that I wanted my children to be happy and not burdened with my life mistakes. Whether they could benefit from my spiritual practice was not readily apparent to me. I did not try to force them to follow my own desires.

My parents had certain expectations of me and wished me to pursue a particular life path, but I was not so inclined. Therefore, my basic premise was to let my own children find their purpose in life, their own paths.

When they were young, they had to accompany me and my late wife to attend the spiiritual events that we participated in. They were initiated into Kriya Yoga practices when they were old enough but we did not force them to take up a sadhana if they did not care to do so.

I believed in parenting by example, which of course was double edged since they could see our committment to following a spiritual practice and yet the results were still a work in progress. They could see that we were quite imperfect and not yet able to demonstrate the benefits of our practice.

In my case, I learned to be a passable parent only when my children were adults.

Practice and Work Tradeoff

Normally, it is possible to balance one's practice and work and still have a fruitful family life. However, under certain circumstances, it might become more and more difficult.

I started out working as an electronics engineer and that suited me very well because I just wanted to earn enough money to support myself and a family. Doing design work in the backroom was exactly what I wanted. I could focus on work during work hours and then meditate at home. Project schedules were the only pressure points and I needed to make little effort to satisfy my management.

Unfortunately, my work karma was very good, in the sense that, in spite of my lack of ambition, I was consistently up for promotion - first into engineering management and then to marketing and finally into business management. Every step on this trajectory required greater commitment to work and provided less time for anything else.

By the time that I met Master, I was chest deep in managing a technology business unit worth several hundred million dollars. It required long hours, lots of traveling and high pressure. It felt like I was caught on a fast-moving carousel that I could not get off.

Once I started my regular spiritual practice with Master, it became apparent to me that it required a higher level of commitment than I was able to make due to my work. I had an epiphany and decided to prioritize my practice. What did this entail?

I would skip lunches and practice in my car or on a park bench. Of course, this didn't work when we had lunch meetings. There were many occasions that I would skip out on intra-company business dinners which are very important for networking and moving higher in a company hierarchy. In the many business meetings, I would not volunteer and take the initiative when someone in my position would do so. Such behavior would tend to sabotage one's career.

An example of prioritization is on a trip to Munich to visit an important customer, we arrived during Oktoberfest, which is a crazy time. After the day-long meeting, we went back to our hotel which was filled with noisy revelers. Our customers had invited us out to one of the tents where they would be drinking beer all night. I declined the invitation and stayed in my room and did my sadhana.

Of course, the work environment has changed a lot since I retired in 2003. There is a lot of acceptance about the benefits of meditation and there is less jeopardy for someone who may be tagged as unambitious. Hopefully, it is now easier to balance one's spiritual and material life.

Personal Transformation

It is generally best to focus on one's practice rather than on the effects of the practice, in order not to get distracted by passing phenomena. However, with the advent of higher consciousness and greater awareness, it is inevitable that one will notice the changes.

A consequence of higher awareness is the stronger connection to our True Self, the presence of which is often described as the Watcher. We become abler to perceive the play of mind-stuff, the arising and submerging of thoughts, as well as even the thought forms themselves in higher states.

With the perception of thoughts, one begins to have greater control over one's emotional reactions. The chain of cause and effect becomes visible and no longer hidden behind emotional clouds. A sense of calmness descends. Of course, there will still be occasions of lesser awareness when self-control slips, but these lapses become less and less.

There comes a greater degree of discernment – the discrimination of right and wrong. The cloud of ignorance can be pierced through and the play of maya temporarily dispersed. A deep and abiding joy accompanies one's discernment.

In the day-to-day world, one is less and less affected by the attractions and aversions of materiality and a strong state of dispassion develops. Emotional states now are equalized, and one begins to live a life of equanimity, free from attachments. A state of freedom to live and love.

From dispassion to equanimity to tranquility. Be at ease, peaceful and free.

> Remember we come from One
> Realize that we are always in One
> Let us live our lives in the One
> In time, we joyfully return to that One.

Rudra Shivananda

The truly enlightened chooses compassion
There is no personal liberation when others suffer
Abandoning the duality of bondage and liberation
Strive to help all beings overcome the life-death cycle

Part 3
Acharya

Rudra Shivananda

Live a new life awakening
Drink deeply of divine nectar
Delight in truth enlightening
Abide in serenity and joy
Upholding wisdom's scepter

Seva

Over the years with Master, besides the Kriya practice, the most important and useful spiritual virtue that I learned is that of seva, or service. There were also interesting experiences during our service.

In the early days, we were hosting him in our home and I was often tasked with driving him to and from the event locations. This minor seva was really quite instructive because having Master next to you in a car can be an extremely powerful experience. He can literally blank my mind without trying to do it. I felt a sense of great accomplishment when I didn't get lost or veer into oncoming traffic which had happened to some of our other sevaks or volunteers. To be able to do things while in the no-mind state is not just a theoretical exercise but becomes a reality when one is working Master.

Time warping is another experience that those of us who've had the privilege of driving Master around marvel at. An example I can recount is one Friday, we had setup a satsang for him in Santa Cruz. This event was scheduled for seven in the evening, and it would normally take about an hour to get there from my house where he was staying. However, it could take an additional twenty minutes or more due to heavy Friday traffic. I had given Master the information and requested that we should be ready to leave around 6 pm. Unfortunately, we didn't leave until 6:40 pm because he needed a rest and a cup of tea to recuperate from an important work he had just finished. I was quite flustered, because this was before the advent of cellphones and I couldn't tell the ground team to let them know that we would be late. We soon encountered heavy traffic and I got even more concerned. Master just laughed and said there was nothing to worry about and it will all be fine. After what seemed like hours, we finally arrived. When I actually looked at my watch, it was only 7:30 pm - not too late at all, as we usually had music, an introduction and a wait for late arrivals. I was surprised because I had expected to arrive after 8 pm.

In the yogic tradition, service to one's Master is a pre-requisite to become worthy of receiving his teachings. Seva helps to remove one's egocentric tendencies. To realize one's True Self, one needs to put aside one's ego-self. We are not used to doing things for others. Whether it is little things like making tea for him in the morning or ironing his clothes, the blessings from such actions are incalculable. We just feel in our hearts that seva to the SatGuru removes a lot of our karmic burden.

Paradoxically, there can often occur competition among the students to offer seva, which sometimes can lead to inflated egos.

All of master's events are organized and managed by volunteers or sevaks. Instead of hiring professionals, he allows us amateurs to handle everything in order to provide a field of service for us to work out our karma. I had the privilege for more than twenty-five years of organizing many of his events in the USA and it has been very spiritually beneficial for me, in spite of the many challenges with logistics and personnel conflicts.

Service is a major theme in my life as my upbringing as a Sikh gave great emphasis to seva as helping those in need regardless of religion, race or caste. In high school, I found great satisfaction in community service. Later, I learned and then gave different healing modalities in an effort to help those who were suffering. Now, as a spiritual teacher, I am committed to sharing Kriya Yoga as the ultimate solution to the suffering of my fellow brothers and sisters.

It cannot be emphasized more that there is no better spiritual training then seva. In the Bhagavad-Gita, a three-wheeled vehicle is used to traverse the spiritual path to enlightenment and liberation from wheel of life and death. The three wheels are the yogas of action, devotion and knowledge. The yoga of action is called Karma Yoga and seva is a practice of this yoga, in which one will offer up the fruits of one's actions to the Divine. Selfless action is the ultimate liberation of the law of cause and effect which binds us to this world of suffering. It complements and enhances the practice of Kriya Yoga.

Expanding Mind and Breaking Barriers through Service

Master is continuously challenging us not just spiritually but also in the material world. He does not always ask the most qualified person to do a particular task but expect us to step up and learn to do what is needed. However, he was not shy to point out our weaknesses either. He expected us to excel and represent him in the best light possible for the sake of getting through to those brothers and sisters who are looking for him but not finding him because he was not well-known, and we did not have funds to do the kind of advertising necessary.

From 1994 to 2002, I was the primary host for Master when he visited the SF Bay area and, consequently, he spent a lot of time with me when I was not at work. It also meant that I was often called upon to do the tasks that he felt was necessary.

First Hamsa Website

Around 1994, I had been reading the technical journals about the internet and the development of business and personal websites being enabled by the availability of a language called HTML. There was also something called a web browser from Netscape that made navigating the net less of a burden.

My history with the internet went back to the 1980s when I was working at National Semiconductor and we had Unix-based computers that used IBM mainframes to communicate throughout our distributed offices across the globe. This was when ARPANET, the defense network, was changed to the TC/IP protocol. By the early 1990s, I was immersed in the memory chip and Intellectual Property business and did not keep in touch with the internet evolution until around 1994, when I was working for VLSI Technology which made semi-custom chips for all the major computer manufacturers.

Master intuitively knew that people would be able to access information through this internet and that it would be useful to have a website. I did more research and, by 1995 was ready to proceed with a primitive website called 'hamsa-yoga.org'. Master spent a lot of time in 1996 fine-tuning the appearance of the website as well as the information. He was particularly fastidious about fonts and images. Master was very much a hands-on Web Guru and a consummate wordsmith. Unfortunately, I was an inept pair of hands, and this was exacerbated by the slower-than-a-turtle dial-up modem I had access to, because it required an exorbitant amount to get a T-1 line that would improve speeds.

For the next few years, I was the webmaster for the site, and it was not until around 2003 that we were able to recruit another Hamsa to take over the role. Master forged a strong sense of the importance of words and images in me that has served me well in everything that I have done since.

Organizing Events

There were only a handful of us who were tasked by Master to be the organizers of his events in the US. In the early days, events were primarily in the SF Bay Area and Los Angeles / San Diego areas. There were three categories of events:

- Satsangs – larger events open to everyone and often with free admission or a token donation. In these Satsangs, Master would talk and answer questions in his own inimitable way as well as give profound experiences to often unready spiritual seekers.

- Kriya Workshops – these were for those who wanted to

commit to a spiritual practice based on the specific Kriya Yoga that Master taught by the grace of Mahavatar Babaji.

- Retreats – these were unforgettable opportunities to spend more time with Master and practice the basic Kriya sadhana as well as receive higher techniques that he deemed suitable from time to time.

The USA tours were always a stressful time because of high expectations and less than satisfactory execution. Most of us were working full-time and volunteering in our diminishing spare time. We did not complain because we were fully aware of the awesome responsibility for organizing events for reaching out to the millions who were seeking for spiritual direction.

We also had the opportunity to provide seva at the events themselves. I was most often called upon to give a small introduction that would help the unprepared attendees to receive the spiritual and healing benefits. The more that I gave these introductions that tried to use Master's words, the more that I felt his Presence within me and all around the event hall. It soon became apparent to me that we can be repeater stations for his transmissions if we can tune to him and let go of our own egos temporarily.

Advertising

There were also many opportunities to learn and improve my graphic capabilities using the very primitive programs of the time in order to provide advertising copy and images to print magazines to promote Master's tour.

One humbling experience that I still recall was the result of not compensating for the poor paper and print quality of a local magazine – a very dark image of Master that he would always later give as an example of poor graphics skill to new sevaks.

Editing and Publishing

One of my life's passions is books - not just reading but collecting fine old books. It never occurred to me that Master would lead me to edit, publish, and even write books.

It all started with him showing me his books of poetry, which he had printed in India. He told me that he wanted to have one published in the US, to include some of his newer poems. However, it was very difficult to find a publisher willing to invest in a book of spiritual poetry by an unknown author.

After some investigating, I bought some software called Pagemaker and found a printing company that would print a book with a minimum of 250 copies. With Master's help, I was able to successfully complete the file for the book, 'Dew Drops of the Soul' and get it printed so that it was made available for our community of spiritual seekers in 2002.

Encouraged by my experience with the Dew Drops of the Soul, I volunteered to edit and publish one of the spiritual treasures of modern times - Master's book, 'Wings to Freedom.' This classic had been in progress for a couple of years, with multiple volunteers helping in the role of stenographers, since Master dictated most of the book and did not put pen to paper as such. He would sometimes have two students with their computers typing away while he was talking. Other times, someone would have a cassette recorder ready while he talked and later another volunteer would transcribe it.

It was challenging to edit all these various bits and pieces of a spiritual masterpiece and sit down with Master to organize them into chapters and subsections. By the end of 2002, I felt that it was complete, and Master arranged on my next visit to India to provide the files to his printer. It was my first time to be spend time in a large off-set printing facility – the environment was quite toxic because of the chemicals used, and we had to spend hours there to get it started. An initial print run of 1500 copies was ordered and one week later, it was ready. I was excited to see the result and we went to the facility again, but to my chagrin, the printer had no quality assurance flow, and it was up to me to check every one of the books. It took more than a day, but we had to reject about four hundred books because of visible printing and binding flaws.

But we were very happy to have over a thousand books and Master did a small puja and prayer to Shiva-Goraksha-Babaji as a blessing. All the books of this first printing were blessed as well.

Although these copies were shipped back to me and made available to the US community in 2004, the journey of this book was not completed until 2009. Master made changes almost every year and the cover design itself changed three times. It gave many of my fellow students opportunity to work with Master to make changes. This was valuable for their spiritual development, as it had been to mine.

Acharya

Master had just finished an event in the SF Bay Area in the late summer of 1998 and we were looking forward to taking off for a late dinner after packing up. Only a few of the close students/organizers were hanging around. Master asked us to stay back and then called us up on the stage. We sat around him.

He started off by telling us that he had decided to setup an order of teachers to help him spread the teachings of Hamsa and Kriya Yoga. As usual when we are around him, we were in still mind and didn't react much. He said that there would be three levels of members - the Sevaks who are the helpers and who can teach the entry practices such as Surya Yoga, the Hamscharyas who will teach the practices of Hamsa Yoga, and the HamsaKriyacharyas who will be authorized to teach both the Hamsa Yoga as well as the Kriya Yoga techniques.

Even though he had briefly talked about doing something like that in the past, I was quite surprised and bemused when he actually called me up and told me that he was going to invest me as a HamsaKriyacharya. He then put his mantle (the white shawl that he always wore) on me and then invested me with sacred power. It was intense and powerful beyond my expectations.

Later, I told Master that I didn't really think that I was qualified to have such an exalted position, but he assured me that I should trust and rely on the connection with him and everything will be fine.

A year or so later, one of the other groups that I belonged to wanted me to become a teacher and suggested that I take a teaching name. This was not something that was strange to me because I had chosen a baptismal name as well as a confirmation name when I joined the Catholic Church in Berkeley. Later, I also had a Buddhist name when I joined the Sangha. While meditating about this, a name came to me that struck a chord within me – Rudra Shivananda. Rudra is the wrathful aspect of Lord Shiva and seemed to evoke my practice to dissolve the ego, while Shivananda is the bliss from the jiva (individual soul) merging with the Divine (Shiva). When Master came for his annual tour, I requested that he bless me with the name, which he did.

Experiences as a Teacher

It is a great blessing to be able to share spiritual teachings and techniques to help our fellow seekers on the path. It is an even greater blessing to be able to connect with a being of Master's spiritual stature when one is engaged in transmitting yogic treasures.

The most important lesson that I learned as a teacher is to put the students' interest ahead of our own in order to faithfully transmit the teachings. One should put aside one's ego and sense of accomplishment. This is best accomplished by offering up ourselves to the divine and connecting heart-to-heart with the divine master within each of us. This divine master is represented in the world in the form of the SatGuru. Without the external SatGuru's guidance, it is possible to be led astray by our own refined and subtle ego when relying on the inner Guru alone. The external SatGuru has awakened the inner Guru within each of us, but we are still not perfected enough to abide in our innate nature.

The effect of teaching while connected with Master is equivalent to being raised to a higher consciousness. With every breath, we breathe in love and breathe out peace. Insights and higher wisdom come pouring in through the connection, as well as past life experiences and teachings. It is not something that can be explained, but needs to be experienced for one to be convinced of the reality. Once one has absorbed the teachings and practices as well as integrated them with their background of spiritual knowledge, one is ready to teach. Most of the time, I connect with Master and find no need to prepare for the teaching sessions, letting go of the need to control, and letting the flow guide me. Answers to questions that I have not even thought about flow out spontaneously. I feel like a river that is connected to an ocean where the water can flow upstream.

I was able to travel and meet with many spiritual people in diverse cultures and countries. For a few years, I was teaching not only the yogic treasures from Master but also valuable yogic techniques from other yogic groups that I had joined and been authorized to teach. Many students became friends and organizers for my workshops. Sometimes, a translator would be needed when English was not the main language, such as in Spain, Japan, Brazil, Russia or Estonia. I found it easier to have direct interaction with students in UK, Ireland, Singapore, Malaysia and USA. Another interesting perspective was visiting different regions within a country. My best cultural experiences have been in different areas of Spain, such as Valencia, Coruna in Galicia, Bilbao, Catalonia and Madrid. The people and food are amazing as well as the spiritual centers – I went into spontaneous paravasta in the Cathedral de Santiago, one of the holiest Catholic churches.

One of the satisfying duties of an acharya within the Siddhanath Yoga Parampara is to support the student community in the US. Most of those who come to Master are advanced souls and it is satisfying to give a helping hand during the retreats by providing revision classes. As Master often reminds us, a SatGuru transforms, while a teacher informs.

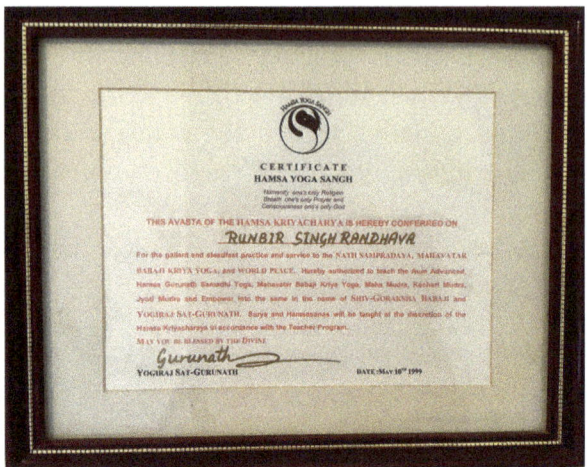

Figure 31a
Acharya certificate from Master

Figure 31b
With Master and other Acharyas at the Ashram

*Figure 32a
Answering questions from students*

*Figure 32b
In Estonia
[the Valley of
Flowers]*

*Figure 32c
Speaking at a
Yoga Festival*

Figure 33a
In Sao Paulo, Brazil

Figure 33b
In Ekaterinberg, Russia

Figure 33c
In Birmingham, United Kingdom

Figure 34a
In Kuala Lumpur,
Malaysia

Figure 34b
In Hong Kong

Figure 34c
In Singapore

*Figure 35a
Teaching during one of
Master's events*

*Figure 35b
Teacher
Training*

*Figure 35c
Giving an introduction during
one of Master's
events*

Figure 36a Some of the different editions of the book, 'Wings to Freedom'

Figure 36b Discussing edits in a book with Master

Spiritual Evolution

Each of us is a potential star! More than that, each of us is potentially Divine, and can hold galaxies in the palm of our hands. Such are the teachings of the Ancients. We've been brought up to reject such wild concepts. Wealth and position in society are now the desired goals to strive towards. In our hearts, we feel the hollowness of realizing such material aspirations, but nonetheless, we feel constrained to follow these social norms.

Reality as perceived by the sages is much more glorious. The earth itself is but star-dust, born from stellar debris, and is constantly evolving. From the earth we obtain our bodies, and from our star, the Sun, we receive our life-force, our soul.

There is an impetus in earth matter to evolve. The physical aspects of evolution have now become acceptable science because of the dedicated work of pioneers such as Darwin. Few dispute the evolution from single cell toward multi-cell organisms, from invertebrate to vertebrate, from reptiles to mammals. Although the real story is much more complex for scientific comfort and man's role as yet clouded by yawning gaps, it is a helpful analogy to the immensity that is spiritual evolution. The ancient masters of yoga have always recognized and taught evolution. In fact, the goal of these ancient spiritual scientists was to accelerate the evolutionary process.

Psychology recognizes the state of a "normal human" being limited to body and superficial mental consciousness, and yet controlled by the vaster unknown depths of sub- and un- consciousnesses.

Yoga shows how the "individual" body/mental consciousness is only one mode of a vaster framework of evolution to soul consciousness, universal consciousness and finally to naked and empty Being, from which all beings arise.

When human evolution advances to the highest level, the subconscious mind is cleared, ego is dissolved and superconsciousness is awakened. We can accept that ordinary human consciousness is light-years beyond animal consciousness, but fail to realize the gap between superconsciousness and our normal human intellect, logic and reasoning. As physical evoution proceeds, the human body becomes a suitable vessel for higher states of consciousness. There is a relationship between spiritual evolution and physical evolution that is yet to be uncovered.

When the highest level of evolution is not only isolated among a few exceptional individuals, but is prevalent in a society, then that society exists completely in harmony with Nature, beyond technology, religion and violence. This would correspond to the 'golden age' that the mystics of many cultures have talked about.

In the meantime, there are brave individuals who are impatient and unwilling to wait for the slow natural progress of evolution. They are the yogis, the mystics, and spiritual revolutionaries. They work with the subtle energy centers called chakras that are also related to the corresponding centers of consciousness. Whether one calls the goal Self-Realization, Spritual Awakening, Ascension or Buddhahood, the committment is to raise human consciousness.

This progressive raising of consciousness is different from the escapism of individual liberation (moksha) or the elitism of 'belonging to the right religion and being saved'. It applies to all living beings. As Master often reminds us, 'We, the Hamsas are meditated to the furthering of Human Awareness".

The Impact of Experiences on the Kriya Yoga Path

Once you've been initiated into Kriya Yoga, you are given a spiritual practice - a sadhana. As you practice over time, there are three possible outcomes in the short and medium term.

Firstly, there may be no discernible experiences. This is obvious if the initiate doesn't practice, but it is disconcerting for the sincere practitioner. It is important to understand that we all start out life with a unique set of karma. The path towards Self-Realization is not a race where everyone starts from the same place and there is only one winner. We all start at a different place and all of us can 'win' by attaining Self-Realization.

On the path, it is not necessary that the sadhak has some spectacular experiences – it can be just a greater sense of peace and a progressive equanimity of emotion over time leading to breakthroughs in higher consciousness.

On the other hand, we've had students excitedly tell us about their great visions and other experiences and in these cases, one would wonder why they have been blessed with these while others have a more humdrum spiritual life (that is, if you can call great joy and peace of mind mundane.) It is taught by the Masters that those who need a vision will get a vision. Past karma may require that a sadhak acquire a particular siddhi or spiritual power because he or she needs to overcome its attraction prior to progress forward. It is not productive to think about your fellow students and their experiences and comparing them with your own.

One would think that positive experiences will be great motivators for the practitioner to do more, but sometimes, the opposite can occur! Why? Some students have told me that they have been scared by the experiences, even though they are pleasant, and stopped their practice prematurely. It is a wonder what the ego mind can do to preserve its dominance and prevent the soul from overcoming its limitations.

A third situation sometimes can occur where a sincere practitioner can have what she or he considers an adverse effect. It can be emotional, mental or physical problems that get connected in the mind as a consequence of the practice and which stops them from continuing out of fear.

Now, to understand what is happening, one has to keep in mind that the practice of Kriya Pranayama accelerates the appearance of the karmic effects that we have taken into this lifetime, and we may not be able to totally burn up the karma by one's own practice and they have to be partially experienced and that is what is responsible for the effects. The karmic effects can be both positive or negative depending on whether it is 'good' or 'bad' karma that is being accelerated.

A key concept to remember is that no new negative karma is being produced because of the practice and in fact if there is any karma generated, it will be positive. The karma activated is our own past karma and we are responsible for it. Also, the karma has to be lived eventually.

An example given by Kriya Masters is the case where a student had the karma to break his leg two years in the future, but because of his practice, this is mitigated to spraining his leg earlier. Obviously, it is not pleasant, but it is better than the alternative.

Once you've eliminated the possibility that you are practicing incorrectly, then you should relax and continue no matter what happens within reason and using your common sense. Please do make sure that your spinal pain or headache is not due to tension or other mistakes during practice. Don't presume to ascribe problems to the practice or to kundalini rising. This discipline has been verified by thousands of practitioners over hundreds of years and, with good guidance, is safe and effective.

Spiritual Experiences – A Practical Perspective

Frequently, students email and ask about the experiences that they have during their practice. Should one drop the practice and flow with the visions?

Spiritual experiences can be very inspiring and help to validate that one is on the right path. However, such experiences can also be intoxicating and lead to unrealistic expectations.

It is important to keep in mind and constantly in sight the goal of our practice: Self-Realization. The objective of our practices is to remove the obstacles that prevent us from realizing our true nature and, until that is accomplished, one should practice diligently and regularly as prescribed during the start or initiation into the specific path we are on. Any disruption or discontinuation of the practice is a detour from our goal and should not be entertained.

If an experience happens during practice, one should detach from it and continue with the practice. There are many such experiences of lesser or greater significance, but they are all forms of distraction that can take us away from our goals. The only exception would be an ecstatic state of super-consciousness which is a state of awareness that is beyond mundane visions – an experience of this nature is beyond the mind and therefore the five senses and should not be confused with a mental experience. One need not be concerned that there would be confusion between the higher super-conscious experience and the lower mental experience – there is no way to detach from a super-conscious state and such a thought would not even be possible.

There will also be spiritual insights and experiences when one is not actively meditating – during a restful time or even during work. It can happen anytime and is the side-effect of one's regular spiritual practice and past karmic efforts. One should learn from these experiences and give thanks for them. However, one should not form expectations or become addicted to them. One can become obsessed with insights and blissful experiences and try to duplicate them or even imagine them, leading to a negative mind-set if they do not recur. What a shame it would be if someone drops away from their practice because they are not getting the vicarious experience they want!

It is also important not to fall into the trap of developing psychic powers so as to access extra-sensory experiences as these are not the fruit of one's practice and will lead to strengthening the ego, rather than realization of the true self. Psychic experiences are detours from the spiritual path and should be avoided.

Next, I will examine some of the major spiritual milestones which have been discussed by the Masters. Normally, it is not advisable to describe the details of the experiences because it might provide mental obstacles to their individual unfolding. There is also the danger that some spiritual seekers in their over-eagerness might simply imagine the experience in their minds – many have been fooled by their minds.

It is not my intention to be overly cautious about spiritual experiences, but it is my duty to warn against being taken for a ride by the ego-mind. Enjoy yourself, but don't strive for or expect the experiences or try to hold on to them.

Experiences and Realizations – A Deeper Perspective

A realization is a permanent change that stays with you as a result of your spiritual practice or divine grace, whereas experiences are temporary. Many of the 'experiences' that I've shared previously are from this perspective, actually realizations while others had a temporary effect only.

Although experiences are transient, it is not recommended to reject them, as that can strengthen them in a negative way. It is best to witness them from a state of detachment. One should accept these experiences and move on.

There are different experiences, from sudden flashes of inspiration to prolonged visions to psychophysical effects. It is instructional to be aware of mental experiences, as such practice can result in the mindfulness of the mind and the deeper layers of svadhyaya.

If we think of the mind as a flowing river, we can experience the following mental states:

- Fast flowing – rapid thoughts
- Turbulent flow – confused thoughts
- Slowly flowing – concentrated thoughts
- Stillness – hardly any thoughts
- Stillness of Stillness – deeper experience of the no thoughts

Keep in mind the last three states are more and more pleasant and rare, but still only temporary states.

There are also landmark experiences which although temporary, are milestones and indications that one is making progress on the spiritual path:

- Bliss or joy: physical effects such as tingling sensations and pulsations accompanied by flashes of light and joy; feelings of being good and inspired

- Luminosity: one experiences a great amount of energy in body and mind and can accomplish what one wants to do. An all-encompassing mental outlook that builds confidence and light into all activities

- Non-thought: very few thoughts occur but there is an overall quality of stillness. On the downside, this can lead to depression because 'nothing is happening'. On the positive side, it is very easy to be detached from emotional ups and downs and there are few hurdles to spiritual practice. This should not be confused with the previous temporary mental states of stillness or even the Stillness of Stillness, which are very short term, while this state of non-thought or no-mind is long-lasting.

Although these landmark experiences are important, they are still not permanent and should not be confused with realizations such as Self-Realization or God-Realization which are totally transformational. These realizations are accompanied by states of bliss, light, no-mind and higher samadhi states such as nirvikalpa samadhi. The ultimate goal is the state of Kaivalya which is a non-dual state of universal unity.

Grief

One of the most difficult experiences that a human being, whether a spiritual practitioner or not, has to process is the death of a loved one. I was devastated by the sudden passing away of my spouse of almost thirty years. It took me over four years to reach the stage of full acceptance. The question arises whether one should let go of the stormy emotions and detach from them earlier using yogic meditations. I decided to let the normal grieving process proceed on the premise that it might otherwise leave long lasting karmic scars or samskaras. Another factor was that I felt that was more respectful of her and our relationship.

However, there are several negative emotions that one should detach from as soon as possible during the grieving process because they pollute the genuine grief. These are blame, shame, and guilt. Whether blaming oneself or others or the divine, there is no positive result and it can only lead to bitterness or a distrust of life. Shame occurs from a feeling of unworthiness while guilt accompanies survival - why one dies and another does not? Awareness of these emotions and detaching from them during meditation is an important part of self-healing.

A blessing throughout the grieving process was that, based on my practice of vairagya or dispassion, I was able to have a deeper appreciation of being 'the watcher.' It's a state where I'm in tears because of a particular poignant memory, but still able to perceive another part of myself being uninvolved.

Books have been written about how to prevent descent into depression after the loss of a dear one. It is not my intention to gloss over the complexities of human reactions. My main point is to let the sincere practitioner know that it is okay to grieve and not be ashamed of one's emotions even though one is aspiring to achieve a tranquil state of equanimity. Naturally, one should continue one's sadhana even in the midst of grief – that is the perseverance that is necessary.

Soon after her passing, several of my fellow students approached me to let me know that she had appeared to them and wanted me to know that she was fine and that I should move on. Master himself also assured me that her soul's journey was positive, and I need not worry. He also performed a fire-ceremony to help her overcome any obstacles. I think the major source of grief for me was that I missed her and the precious love we shared.

> Grief love loss tears fall
> Heroic heart helpless pall
> Let go baseless blame
> Let go silent shame
> Let go gnawing guilt
> Honor shining soul flight
> Cherish shared joy delight

Siddhanath Yoga Parampara

Over the years, Master has developed and taught many different spiritual and healing techniques to help his students to make rapid progress. Sometimes, he decides that some techniques were too advanced or some were not powerful enough and he would make changes or remove them completely. He is never stuck in the past and always ready to innovate for the sake of his students.

It is instructive to understand the difference between the term sampradaya and parampara. Sampradaya refers to a school of teaching or philosophy such as the Nath Sampradaya or teachings of the Naths. Parampara specifically refers to a chain of SatGurus that best represent the spiritual lineage. In this case, the lineage is from Mahavatar Babaji to Yogiraj SatGurunath Siddhanath, but since Babaji is too vast and is the initator of many lineages, our lineage is named Siddhanath Yoga Parampara.

After much experimentation, he established a system that he felt suitable to the present times. This consisted of three complementary and one core system:

- Kundalini Kriya Yoga is the core system for Self-Realization
- Hamsa-Surya which includes the Siddhanath Surya Yoga as supplementary techniques for physical, emotional and mental purification and transformation
- Siddhanth Shakti Healing for overcoming obstacles to spiritual practice
- Advanced Benefactor techniques that accelerate spiritual growth for those who are attending longer residential camps with Master

Rudra Shivananda

The Healing Power of the Sun

One of Master's great contributions is the spreading of peace in the world by demonstrating the unity in humanity with the timeless gifts of our common ancestor, the Sun. He developed the **Siddhanath Surya Yoga** to re-connect us to the great benefactor, teacher and ruler of our solar system. There are now many Surya Hamsa teachers throughout the world who help to spread these healing methods.

We have realized that this is a time of transition and turbulence. There is a breakdown in social and personal security. With increasing polarization and distrust among nations and peoples, there is mounting violence and bloodshed in this fragile ecosystem we call Earth. A philosophy of peace, both world and personal, must be based on unity, rather than differentiation. It is now imperative that all of us understand the common bonds between all peoples. The great spiritual paths have all taught that the solution to the world's problems is to transcend the restrictive personal ego and realize the higher dimensions of humanity - the essential one-ness underlying our individual experiences.

There is a common bond among all beings on Earth. All life is based on and sustained by the great Light of the Sun. It is an indisputable scientific fact that there would be no life on Earth without the Sun. Our Sun gives its life-force and light to all beings on Earth, regardless of race, gender, and beliefs. The rich and the poor are treated equally by the Sun. Those who act positively and those who act negatively are equally embraced by the light and love of this visible representation of the invisible Divine cosmic Love and Light.

There is no higher visible connection to the universal life-force than compassionate *Surya* [one of the many Sanskrit *Vedic* names of the Sun]. There is no greater source of healing and purification for humanity. Throughout the ages, all peoples have looked up to the Sun in love and gratitude for the gift of life. Some, propelled by dark ignorance, have distorted their 'worship' with self-serving and humanity-hating practices, while others have been led to ignore this visible representation of the invisible creator. It is a tragic fact that in no other time in humanity's past, have so many lost their connection with the Sun, as in the modern era.

When the power of Surya is invoked, it is not only the physical form of the Sun that is to be accessed, but the energetic and spiritual essence. Humanity has been endowed, not only with a physical form, but also with energetic, emotional, mental, and spiritual aspects. Even plants have feelings, so with what arrogance and ignorance do the children of the Sun consider their creative agent to be only a non-sentient fireball?

When a spiritual seeker makes a connection with the Sun, he or she will heal the physical body, acquire greater vitality, overcome all negativity, and also come to a greater understanding and realization of one's true nature.

The real nature and significance of the Sun has always been realized and taught by the true saints and seers of all cultures, especially by the ancient yogis of India. The great spiritual classics, such as Vedas and Upanishads all sing the praises of the Sun, the light, and the fire, as witness, friend and sustainer of all life. There is continuity from those ancient days to the current fast-paced, technologically driven culture – the Sun, Light and Fire are still praised everyday by millions in India. Tragically, much of the knowledge in other parts of the world have been lost or suppressed by neo-religious fanatics over the last several millennia.

Solar techniques and practices transcend and do not belong to any religion and are not religious practice in the usual narrow use of the term. However, they do help to open the practitioner up to a more profound and higher dimension of awareness and experience and are spiritual from that perspective. Regular practice will help one feel the unity and harmony of all life.

There is a trite, but nonetheless true, saying that "familiarity breeds contempt" and, sadly, humanity has often fallen prey to this fault in our psyche, even applying it to the greatest of beings in our solar system, the Sun. Modern humanity no longer give thanks to the bringer and sustainer of life, and think ourselves superior to our ancestors, who stood in awe of manifest divinity.

The ancient yogis did not worship 'gods' as we now understand this concept. They sang in joy and gratitude to the Divine, which they "saw and experienced" as manifesting in different 'light beings' or devas. These ancient rishis in their cosmic enlightenment, sang praises to the principle of Light, by manifesting their unitary state in pluralistic thoughts, words and deeds, for the sake of seekers after the Truth.

These Vedic seers spoke in symbols of Light to awaken the internal Light in the heart of every being. To these Masters of life and death, the Sun or Surya is the symbol of the enlightened mind, the true Self, free from the darkness of ignorance.

Many names are used to describe the many aspects of the Sun in the Vedas, and it is instructive to look at the meanings attached to some of these:

Surya:	Universal Soul, Great Witness
Savitar:	Creator, Great Transformer
Mitra:	Divine Friend
Varuna:	Infinite Space, Great Peace
Aditya:	Light
Vishnu:	That which Pervades
Pushan:	Great Sustainer

The Sanatana Dharma or Eternal Way is the Solar transformation of darkness to light. The outer Sun is the visible representation of the inner light of transformation present in every human being.

For the Western World, the most defining time of the last millennia was the end of the 'Dark Ages', heralded by the efforts of Galileo and Copernicus to put the Sun in its rightful place. Putting the Sun back in the center of our solar system started the Age of Enlightenment! Let us now begin the process of putting the Sun back in its rightful place in the center of our lives and start the Age of Self-Realization.

The Siddhanath Surya Yoga developed by Master is a panacea for our times. It is not only energizing and healing - it has aspects that accelerates spiritual evolution - a true transformative practice.

Embrace the light of our soul

To illuminate the darkness of mind

Surya, you are the rainbow bridge

Leading us through Maya to our goal

Siddhanath Kriya Yoga

Kriya Yoga was introduced in modern times by Mahavatar Babaji through Lahiri Mahasaya. There are now many different streams of Kriya Yoga, due to the passage of time and the needs of students as perceived by the various Kriya Masters.

In Part 1, I briefly outlined some of the features of Kriya Yoga in general. Now, specifically, what Master teaches is, to my understanding, an advanced form that will provide a boost to practitioners.

He has incorporated the Omkar Kriya into the Basic Kriya Sadhana, thereby healing the chakras earlier than the systems taught by other groups. Another improvement is the strengthening of the mantras used during the Kriya Pranayama as well increasing the number of repetitions. Thirdly, the formal relationship between the number of mahamudras and the number of pranayamas performed is very beneficial to breaking through energy blocks quickly.

For our purpose, I will focus on the process of Kriya Yoga in awakening and raising the nascent Kundalini energy from its potential into kinetic form through the first six chakras and onward to the thousand petalled lotus at the top of the crown. From this perspective, the basic practice is as follows:

- Omkar Kriya: this restores and heals the chakras in order for them to convert and store more prana as well as removing the karmic blockages that prevent full functioning. A strong store of prana is required for the Kundalini Shakti to transform from its potential to kinetic state. There is also an Advanced Omkar Dhyana that incoporates the visualization of the petals of the each of chakras.
- Shiva-Shakti Anusandhana: this is the Kriya Pranayama that opens up the blocked central channel (sushumna nadi) which

is a requirement for the ascendence of the kundalini.

- Mahamudra: this integral practice helps to raise the kundalini through the right pathway.
- Paravasta: this the state of rest after the dynamic portion of the sadhana and is the opening up to the transcendental state of pure consciousness.

Once the basic foundation is established through the above sadhana, the practitioner can add on advanced techniques to it. The purpose of these advanced techniques is to speed up the removal of karmic blockages.

There are three blocks called granthis which are especially troublesome - the first one at the naval center connected with the material world, the second at the heart center, connected with the emotional plane, and the last at the third-eye center dealing with the manifestation of ignorance and illusion itself. The Advanced Kriyas are:

- Nabho Kriya: for cutting the knot at the naval center
- Vishnu Granthi Bhedan: for cutting the knot at the heart center
- Jyoti Mudra (a more advanced form is called Shiva-Netra Bhedan): for cutting the karmic knot at the third-eye center

There are other supplementary practices that can be added as well. However, every practice that is added will increase the time needed for the sadhana. It is better to practice deeply rather than superficially by accumulating a lot of techniques.

Rudra Shivananda

Guidance on Kriya Yoga

An important responsibility of being a teacher is to answer questions from our students. It is humbling but also gives great satsifaction to be of some help to fellow students on the path. Although we cannot explore details about Kriya Yoga because of its sacred transmission aspect, there are certain important questions that are general in nature that may be helpful for those who are considering taking up this path or have recently started.

Is Kriya Yoga a Religion?

The practice of yoga can be very confusing for students, especially those from the West, because of the frequent use of terms and concepts which are common with Indian religious systems. However, one needs to differentiate the same words used in different contexts. A term may be used to represent an abstract concept, a spiritual principle or a function in yoga. The same term can be used to describe the powers or divine figures in religion.

Shiva represents the power of dissolving the practitioner's ego in yogic meditation whereas Lord Shiva is one of the three main dieties of the Indian Religions.

Another even more fundamental difference between yoga and a religion is the reliance of one's own experience versus the experience of the religion's founder or a particular scripture. Yoga is concerned with one's own state of consciousness. The practitioner's goal is to realize the state of consciousness of Lord Shiva, of the Christos, and of the Lord Buddha.

The yogic practitioner is not content to read about what the great spiritual giants have attained or what great deeds they performed, but to tread their path and follow their example.

The prayer of the yogic practitioner is to their own True Self, the Inner Guide, the Atman, the Spirit Within.

Do you need to be vegetarian to practice Kriya Yoga?

It is commonly understood that non-harming other beings in thought, word or deed is a mark of a spiritual person. There is a long tradition of vegetarianism in India based on the premise that eating meat violates the injunction not to harm any living thing. Therefore, one's diet has taken up a lot of interest among those who practice the spiritual path.

We can certainly agree that the vegetarian life-style is healthly from the viewpoint of introducing less chemicals and hormones into one's body. The meat industry often uses artificial means to fatten the animals in the shortest period of time to decrease their cost and increase profits.

The karmic consequences of killing animals is also undisputed. No doubt, being vegetarian will incur less bad karma. Incuring more bad karma is harmful for one's spiritual life. Even if one can rationalize that the animal is being butchered professionally and not personally, we are encouraging these acts of cruelty.

On the other hand, it has been proved that even vegetables are capable of feeling and the eating of a salad is not free from karmic consequence either. We may be able to rationalize that there is a lower order of karma involved in the killing of lettuce versus the killing of a chicken, but it's only a matter of degree.

In order to encourage regular people to take up the spiritual path, Master has often reminded us that human beings are all part of the food chain together with the rest of the Earth's inhabitants, whether animal or plant. We have to eat to survive.

It may not be very important whether one eats meat or vegetables in the grand scheme of things. We incur more karma by every thought or word or action that we continously expose to the world. All the negative and harsh words that we speak may be more harmful than the salmon that we had for dinner.

From the perspective of a meditator, it is immediately possible to experience the effect of a few days of moving to a vegetarian diet - the mental states are much steadier with fewer and calmer thoughts. When we eat pork or beef for a few meals, there is a notable increase in the passionate nature of the mental states - higher agression or more fearful. We can experience for ourselves that eating fish or seafood instead can lead to a more controlled meditation because of the lower intensity of their emotional energies.

The reason for the difference in the quality of meditation can be attributed to the theory that when we eat something, we are not only digesting the fats, protein and carbohydrates but also the emotional nature of the food. In our yogic model, human beings have an energetic, emotional, mental and karmic bodies, in addition to the physical. In the same way, animals and plants have energetic and emotional bodies.

Whether one is a vegetarian or a meat eater, the only way to overcome the cycle of birth and death is by achieving Self-Realization. One does not achieve liberation by being a vegetarian, nor are you prevented from successfully achieving enlightenment if you are not vegetarian.

Decreasing meat in one's diet and moving from red meat to chicken or fish will have a beneficial effect on one's spiritual practice. It is not however, a replacement for regular practice.

Do I have to give up smoking or drinking to practice?

Everyone has certain habits that they may have developed before getting intiated into their sprtual practice. Master does not advocate for the student to spend too much effort in getting rid of the habits that are difficult to remove. Instead, one can should focus on the practice.

The more one practices, the freer one becomes and bad habits can fall off on their own. It is the practice that transforms the student and eventually, the habits become meaningless. If one waits until one has rid oneself of all bad habits first before practicing, how long will it take? Instead of waiting for the perfect time, the perfect place, or the perfect me, just do it.

Self-Inquiry and Self-Criticism

There seems to be confusion about meditation and our innate critical voice. We are all aware to some degree about this inner voice that interrupts our joy with future fears or our plans with uncertainty or over-analyse our mistakes. This power of self-criticism need not be cultivated during your meditation.

Self-inquiry or contemplation is about understanding ourselves, our minds and emotions better in order to overcome our karmic programming. It is not about giving ourselves a tongue lashing or belittling our accomplishments.

We need to let go of our self-criticisms and move forward with constructive changes if necessary. Understanding ourselves better will help us to make less future mistakes, whereas self-criticism provides no behavioural adustments - it only serves to augment guilt or other destructive emotions.

Many seekers shy away from meditation because of this self-critical voice, which is ego-centric and not part of self-study.

Is it dangerous to awaken or raise the kundalini?

There is a lot of misleading literature as well as word of mouth, about the dangers of kundalini. They are mostly without foundation or based on misunderstanding the nature of so-called kundalini experiences.

First of all, there are no dangers in following the guidelines and practices given in Siddhanath Kriya Yoga. These techniques have been proven to be safe for tens of thousands of seekers over hundreds if not thousands of years.

The process of awakening and rasing kundalini is a scientifically formulated process that, if taught and practiced correctly, is safe. The kundalini energy is almost impossible to accidentally awaken - it takes effort, discipline, concentration, and life-force energy to appear. After it appears, the kundalini follows a particular path in the astral spine to rise.

Secondly, what people mistakenly call kundalini experiences are mostly pranic or life-force problems. This life-force energy is also a powerful energy within us and goes through many pathways to nourish our physical, emotional and mental bodies. However, these pathways can be damaged through life-style changes, by accidents or drugs. When their pathways are damaged or blocked, and excessive prana is generated through inappropriate metthods either internally or externally, bad experiences occur.

Thirdly, in modern times, people experiment on their own by reading books, watching videos, or through social media. This is like trying to become a chemist on your own without going to classes or guidance from a qualified chemist - you can imagine the problems that can arise.

GuruMaa

GuruMaa is Master's spouse and spiritual companion. She is also lovingly called Aie or mother because of her caring nature. She exemplifies the nature of Divine Mother.

GuruMaa is truly a great partner for Master. While he is looking after our spiritual welfare, she makes sure that our material needs are met. When I first went to the Siddhanath Forest Ashram, I marveled at the amount of work that she personally undertook. She did most of the cooking with only a few helpers from the local village. She was also the overseer for the local contractors that were handling the continuous maintenance and building projects in the Ashram. It was a very rustic and harsh environment. Without her perseverance and shakti energy, the Ashram of today would probably be non-existent.

Her caring attitude can be shown from a little episode from my first trip to the Ashram and the subsequent Himalayan Pilgrimage. At the end of the pilgrimage, we were at Rishikesh and I needed to get to the Delhi airport to take my return flight back to the California. Everyone else was staying an extra day and I would be the only one traveling to Delhi. GuruMaa was very concerned and decided to go with me on a taxi from Rishkesh to Delhi, an over seven-hour ride in those days, to make sure that nothing untoward would happen.

It was the day of Holi, the festival of colors, and everywhere there were crowds throwing water balloons with colored water inside as well as firing colored powder propellant guns. It was a wild and chaotic scene in all the villages and towns we passed. The taxi driver had trouble navigating in Delhi because he was from the Garwhal region but thanks to GuruMaa's instructions, I actually made it to the airport on time.

Even though GuruMaa is a royal princess of the Marathas that ruled Tamil Nadu from Tanjore for a number of generations, she is an extremely gracious and humble person. However, this does not mean that she is a pushover. She can explode with righteous anger just like Mother Durga and make sure Hamsas are not taken advantage of in India. She can also admonish Master when he sometimes forgets his advanced age and tries to overexert his physical body.

Although I was not there to witness all the work that she put into acutalizing the Ashram in the early days, I was assured by Master that without her hard work and dedication, there would not be a material realization of his spiritual work. I can believe this because, every year that I visited the Ashram, I witnessed the growth and evolution brought about by her constant effort. It was like the Ashram was another of her children that she had given birth to and nurtured. She overcame many hardships, such as lack of funds in the early days and the constant lack of skilled labor.

While everyone else was gathered around Master, she was in the background, making sure there was food for everyone and that the facilities were working.

Another aspect of GuruMaa that oftentimes is forgotten is her high spiritual consciousness. She is so low-key and Master is so forceful that we do not realize that she was also born from an aspect of Divine Mother. Those who are fortunate to help her cook in the kitchen experience meditation in action and maintain a higher consciousness throughout the process. A highlight for many people is the opportunity we get to meditate with her, such as at the Shasta Retreats where we can immerse ourselves in her oceanic consciousness.

Figure 37 GuruMaa with Gurunath - a companion, Annapurna and Shakti

Feeding Master

At the Ashram in 1999

Master's Programs in USA

It is a great blessing that Master is still active in travelling all over the world to give his transformative experiential events. Most of the USA events have been in California, although he has given retreats in Washington and on the East Coast.

A sign of Master's emphasis on the importance of words can be seen from his removal of the word 'retreat' from our lexicon. His events are better described as Life and Livingness Camps.

There are many testimonials from attendees about the life changing experiences that they were graced with during these programs. An especially favorite feature is that of the Dreamweaver in which Master appears in our dreams to remove emotional or mental blockages - a process he calls 'chakra surgery'. He may also work on the deeper levels of our being, in which case we would only feel energetic changes but not have the dream experience.

In a period of thirty years, we have visited many retreat centers in California. In the last six years, our favorite location has been at Mount Shasta, a well-known area with a spiritual and mystical reputation.

During our 2014 event at Shasta, Master took us up to the topmost accesible spot in cars and we meditated there at midnight. When Master started an impromptu satsang, most of us felt the presence of many other beings and some of us saw their extremely tall humanoid figures clustered outside our circle, listening to him. It seems that these beings are those called Lemurians, the remnant of an ancient race that lived on Earth in a bygone age - they live in a certain dimension of Mt. Shasta.

*Figure 38a
A candid moment during a photo session with acharyas*

*Figure 38b
Master giving a blessing to a Hamsa at a USA 'retreat'*

*Figure 39b
Acharya teaching at one of Master's USA 'retreats'*

*Figure 40a
Meditating by the
ocean at Carlsbad*

*Figure 40b
Master performing
a fire-ceremony at
Mt. Madonaa*

*Figure 40c
Master giving
Kriya Empowered Initiation*

*Figure 40d
Relaxing moment on
boat excursion during a
Mt. Shasta 'retreat'*

The Ashram Now

Although we are encouraged by Master to visit pilgrimage sites in other parts of India, there is no doubt in my mind that my favorite place for a spiritual pilgrimage is his own Ashram outside the city of Pune. The connection with Master has hallowed the whole area and there is a palpable difference between being outside and inside, making it very conducive for the practice of Kriya Yoga.

The most important additon to the Ashram since it was established has to be that of the Earth Peace Temple - a unique marble temple without any murti of a divine being. Inside is a solidified mercury shivalinga, the largest akhanda or single piece such structure that we are aware of.

My own experiences meditating in front of the mercury shivalinga has been independently verified by many others at different times. We all felt a steadiness in our minds to the point of being in a thoughtless state. An energy movement in our astral spine is very common. Another experience is the vision of Master himself in the shivalinga.

Meditating with the shivalinga is so popular that during the Mahashivaratri Camp, the attendees have to take turns in order not to overcrowd the temple. A popular seva for the old students is to clean the temple, drain and then refill the water tank around the shivalinga. We are not normally allowed to touch the shivalinga.

A very recent addition is a spiritual pool below the steps to the temple. It has been sanctified for meditation and the practice of Kriya. The use of water is very beneficial to the circulation of prana.

*Figure 41a
Master looking up at the Earth Peace Temple*

*Figure 41b
Master with mercury Shivalinga*

*Figure 41c
Master with Ashram calf*

*Figure 41d
Master and GuruMaa giving Ghosti around the fire*

Figure 42a
My meditation hut in the Ashram

Figure 42b
Gift giving to the children

Figure 42c
Making garlands with other Hamsas at the Ashram

Figure 42d
Walking with Master and his family during Ashram festivities

SatGurunath's Contribution to Yogic Science

Master gives us fresh wisdom directly from the divine source, the fount of all knowledge, Mahavatar Babaji.

- He has revealed that the Mahayogi Gorakshanath who manifested from Lord Shiva himself and Mahavatar Babaji who bestowed Kriya Yoga to humanity are one and the same

- He has identified that the mystical Hamsa is connected with the third ventricle in the brain and the yogic third-eye chakra

- He demonstrated that the differentiated mind of the disciple can be attuned to the undifferentiated consciousness of the Master through Shivapat

- He developed an effective healing and transformational program to harness the power the of the Sun – Siddhanath Surya Yoga

- He personified a householder in order to give confidence to modern men and women that they can achieve Self-Realization following the path of Kriya Yoga

Master's Many Manifestations

From an experiential perspective, those of us who been fortunate to see some of Master's past life connections during the Shivapat will not be surprised that there are photographs that best capture these aspects in the present lifetime.

Master has what is best described as an archetypal face – casual passers-by often stare at him and come up to compliment his Presence. In Italy, they call him Jupiter or Neptune while in other countries they liken him to Moses. He takes it all in good humor because, even though he has come with his being veiled, his light pierces through the disguise.

There are photographs that have, by his grace shown forth his connection with the Sun, with El Morya, Moses, Shri Yukteswar and others. Some students resonate better with particular aspects, which is natural due to past life connections. I've presented a few of them as illustrative of this wonderful phenomenon.

The Uniqueness of SatGurunath

Perhaps it is too trite for a student to laud his or her teacher but nonetheless I must do so despite all derision and doubt for the sake of my fellow brothers and sisters on the path.

All great spiritual teachers are worthwhile subjects of adulation for the wisdom that they are giving. However, I have not found any that can actually demonstrate the facticity of their timeless teachings. It is one thing to say that we are all one or that we are all interconnected, but who is willing or able to show this to us?

Master does not only talk but can walk his talk. In all his public and private sessions, he gives one or more experiences that will help the attendees make substantial progress in their spiritual evolution. The following are the three empowering experiences that he has given to thousands of unprepared souls in order to help them on the path:

- Shaktipat transmission: this is a transmission of kundalini energy that can evolve and/or heal depending on the need and will of the receiver. Master can send this energy in a center to center progression, such as to the naval center, heart center and the third-eye center, or to the whole body.

- Pranapat transmission: this demonstrates the truth that Master often reminds us - "humanity is connected by the self-same cord of breath." This is the true empowerment that only a Kriya Master can give to move the prana in the subtle spine of the disciple. In this experience, Master lengthens our breath, making it longer and deeper and in some cases, breathes for us even when we stop our own breath.

- Shivapat: He lets us share in the outer fringes of his nirvikalpa samadhi so that we can experience the higher consciousness states of sarvikalpa samadhi. This demonstrates we are one in our consciousness.

As far as we know, SatGurunath is the only one who gives such transmissions to the public in these times.

Master is unusual in that he does not stand apart from humanity but actually uses mundane tools to help us. He can connect with his students on different levels, whether as a friend, teacher, Master or Divine Being. He jokes with them or can be stern with them. He can forgive their low understanding and is always looking for ways to help them. For those who are stressed, he would take them to Disneyland for the rides and cotton candy. I've seen how, over the years many students have been healed of long-term problems because of just spending time with Master. He would often take us walking in nature or swimming in the pools, rivers, lakes, and oceans. Connecting with nature is another of his favorite healing methods – this not only heals us but can heal nature as well.

It has been and continue to be a great blessing for me to be guided and transformed by Master. The journey continues in his Presence.

Figure 43a
Iconic Images of SatGurunath

Figure 43b
More Iconic Images of SatGurunath

The Presence

I take refuge in that auspicious Presence
Who removes the worldly bonds that bind us
That giver of true knowledge
Who removes our mayic ignorance

I take refuge in that auspicious Presence
Who is the embodiment of saving grace
That SatGurunath, the perfect guide
Who illuminates our inner precious polestar

I take refuge in that auspicious Presence
Who protects the seed of our essence
That Siddhanath, that pure path of perfection
Who grants us the gifts to pierce our limitations

I take refuge in that auspicious Presence
Who is beyond Divine Mind
That existed before the world manifest
Who skillfully dissolved my illusive ego

Rudra Shivananda

I take refuge in that auspicious Presence
Who protects us from our wayward senses
That Yogiraj, the seer that cures our blindness
Who leads us to abide in natural bliss

I take refuge in that auspicious Presence
Who wakes us from our dreams
That being beyond the states of becoming
Who shows us our true Self to Be

Books by Rudra Shivananda

Chakra selfHealing by the Power of Om

Yoga of Purification and Transformation

Surya Yoga - Healing by Solar Power

Breathe Like Your Life Depends On It

In Light of Kriya Yoga

Healing Postures of the 18 Siddhas

Insight and Guidance for Spiritual Seekers

Practical Mantra Yoga

Breathe Better Live Longer

Nada: The Yoga of Inner Sound

Living A Spiritual Life In A Material World

website: www.rudrashivananda.com
blog: www.sanatanamitra.com
www.youtube.com/user/KriyaNathYogi

About the Author

Rudra Shivananda, a disciple of the Himalayan GrandMaster Yogiraj Gurunath Siddhanath, is dedicated to the service of humanity through the furthering of human awareness and spiritual evolution. He teaches that the only lasting way to bring happiness into one's life is by a consistent practice of awareness and transformation. He has developed healing programs utilizing the energy centers [Chakras] and Prana Energy techniques through breath.

Rudra Shivananda is committed to spreading the message of his Master: "Earth Peace through Self Peace". He teaches this message of World and Individual Peace through the practice of Kriya Yoga. As a student and teacher of yoga for more than 50 years, he is trained as an Acharya or Spiritual Preceptor in the Indian Nath Tradition, closely associated with the Siddha tradition. He lives in the San Francisco Bay area, and has given initiations and workshops in USA, Ireland, England, Japan, Spain, Brazil, Russia, Singapore, Malaysia, Hong Kong, India, Australia, Canada and Estonia.

Transformed by The Presence

www.ingramcontent.com/pod-product-compliance
Lightning Source LLC
Chambersburg PA
CBHW060836170426
43192CB00019BA/2791